# Challenging Behaviour

## A fresh look at promoting positive learning behaviours

**Anne Copley**

Published by
Network Continuum Education
The Tower Building, 11 York Road, London SE1 7NX

www.networkcontinuum.co.uk
www.continuumbooks.com

An imprint of The Continuum International Publishing Group Ltd

First published 2006
© Anne Copley 2006
(with the exception of pages 46–50 (six key motivators concepts) and Chapter 7, Will Thomas)

ISBN-13: 978 1 85539 217 5
ISBN-10:    1 85539 217 8

Managing editor: Janice Baiton
Layout: Marc Maynard – Network Continuum Education
Cover design: Marc Maynard – Network Continuum Education

Printed in Great Britain by MPG Books Ltd, Bodmin, Cornwall

# Contents

# Foreword:
## squids, kids and fishing

In 2004, a rare and elusive giant squid was captured off the coast of the Falkland Islands. It attracted my attention on a number of levels: first, because I have an uncle and aunt who lived and worked in the Falklands for many years; second, because of my fascination with the animal kingdom; third, I was captivated by the sheer mystery of the creature. 'Archie', as he is affectionately known (from his Latin name *Architeuthis dux*), is 8.5 metres (28 feet) long. He is currently residing, pickled in formaldehyde, in a tank in London's Natural History Museum. Very few of these creatures have ever been discovered dead, let alone alive. Archie is not the biggest one ever caught – that accolade belongs to a fishing crew in New Zealand's waters in the late 1800s.

So how is it that such a large creature has remained so elusive over the centuries? The answer probably lies in its habitat. It lives in the southern oceans at depths of more than 1,000 metres (3,280 feet). At these kinds of depths the human body is unable to withstand the pressures of diving without highly specialized equipment. It is a dangerous place, awash with aggressive predators and crushing water pressure. As technology has improved, more has been learned about these mysterious giant squids. Their habits and whereabouts have been tracked with sonar and through the use of increasingly robust diving vessels that can search the highly pressurized depths of the oceans. Collecting direct and indirect evidence of their existence, ecology and physiology has built a fuller picture.

Perhaps a parallel exists between this book and squid hunting. The more we have learned about the structure and mysterious functioning of the human brain, the more teachers have been able to inform their handling of challenging behaviour in schools. It is the reason why, in this book, Anne Copley takes time to update us on developments in behavioural neuroscience. She ably links this to the daily situations we might meet in the classroom. Through reading *Challenging Behaviour*, you will further understand the reasons why young people misbehave at a neurological level and a social level. It is this understanding that reframes our thinking and helps us to take control and regain influence in school.

Down the centuries, the quest of the hunters of the elusive squid has been helped by improved understanding. Knowing the geography and biology of the beast, the likely depths at which it operates and the specific functioning of the animal has enabled hunters to be properly resourced, to predict behaviours and be suitably prepared for the quest. Technology associated with locating and tracking these sea animals has led to increased success in understanding and locating them. In our classrooms and schools, understanding the geography and biology of our students is also helpful in identifying the right solutions to managing their learning behaviour. What Anne has done, in a simple and straightforward way, is to bring the science of behaviour management to the fore. She explains the reasons *why* children behave and misbehave, *what* you need to do and *how* you need to do it, to promote learning behaviours and minimize disruption. The effect is a fully equipped fishing vessel. If you know why your squid behaves as it does, you can predict its behaviour, track its pathway and land it safely in the learning zone. With understanding, you use your strategies with accuracy and appropriateness, rather than fishing blindly in the dark depths of oceans for a highly adapted creature.

I commend this book as a way of not only understanding challenging behaviour but also of considering your own fishing vessel. Few, if any, books on classroom management invite you to consider yourself in the classroom. What Anne does is to safely and comfortably support you to consider what you bring into the room and how this supports good learning behaviours. Knowing how your fishing vessel behaves in all kinds of waters assists you in steering it and its booty of strategies and technologies towards getting the best catch. *Challenging Behaviour* is a high-tech behaviour management approach in low-tech language that we can all understand. This book is the science, the art and the technology of promoting learning, all within one cover.

There is no doubt that working with behaviour that challenges you is tough. However, understanding more about why it happens and how you can deal with it can become enticing, if you can allow it to. To use the full technology of your sonar, your radar, your nets and the understanding of how you handle the vessel, is to catch squid. And that is really satisfying. With a little more knowledge, who knows just how big a squid you can land? Enjoy fishing for squid.

Will Thomas
Performance coach and author
March 2006

# How to use this book

This book has been designed to provide you with just enough of what you need to get you where you want to go. With this in mind, the text is organized with the theory followed by practical suggestions. There are three sections that focus on:

- the 'Why?', which explores why we need to approach behaviour management from an understanding of human physiology and behaviour.
- the 'What?', which explores what we need to do to proactively encourage positive learning behaviours.
- the 'How?', which explores how to build and maintain learning behaviours and how to intervene when things do not go according to plan. This part also explores an often-forgotten element of classroom management – the teacher's own health and well-being. Here you are helped to develop ways to better meet your needs. Managing stress and coping strategies for the challenging role of teaching today are explored.

Within each chapter you will find:

- mind maps summarizing content
- a list of what you will learn in the chapter
- preview questions to help activate your learning
- example dialogues and case studies where appropriate
- summary points reviewing the main content
- self-coaching insight questions.

This means you can read the book in a number of ways. You could:

- start at the beginning and work methodically through the book.
- read the chapter outcomes first and then dip in.
- read the chapter summaries first.
- consider the chapter preview questions as a guide.
- use the book as a reference using the tools in section 3.
- use the book as a personal and professional development experience by working through the self-coaching questions at the end of each chapter.

Challenging Behaviour – A fresh look at promoting positive learning behaviours

# Acknowledgements

There is no doubt that if I had not met Will Thomas, this book would never have been written. While the content is the culmination of many years enjoying the day-to-day challenge of learning with all manner of adults and young people, it has been Will's absolute faith in my work and his ability to coach me into believing that I had something worthwhile to say that has resulted in this book.

In addition to providing the inspiration for me to write, Will has also made contributions to the content of this book in the form of 'the six key motivators' concepts in Chapter 4 and the entirety of Chapter 7, Self-coaching and maintaining your own sanity.

For almost 30 years I have been researching, reading, listening, watching and experimenting. Through this book I have a chance to share this more widely.

It would prove impossible to mention the hundreds of people who have supported and inspired me over the years. My apologies to any I forget to mention but here are a few:

- Janette Maude for keeping faith in me and ensuring I stayed in touch with reality.
- Anna Collinge for never doubting my commitment when so many were challenging me, and her husband, Mark Collinge, for sorting out my accounting system.
- Adele Beeston for being such an inspirational teacher and supporting my work at Oakgrove.
- Alistair Smith and all his team at Alite, especially Kim Pemberton, for giving me the chance to get in front of so many people and share these approaches.
- All the headteachers who have allowed me to work with their staff and have so much fun, especially Louise Tunstall and the Sutton heads.
- All those pupils and parents who have called a 'spade a shovel' and provided me with such an insight into real life.

My grateful thanks goes to Julie Thomas for producing a 'concept cover' that helped to shape the eventual cover of the book.

Finally, the most important influence in my life, my partner, Sue, who has remained absolutely by my side through some pretty dark times, always supporting what I needed to do, even when I had no idea what I was doing. I could never have taken the opportunities I have without her quiet, solid yet challenging support. She has allowed me to become more than I ever believed I could be.

# Section 1

## Why manage learning?

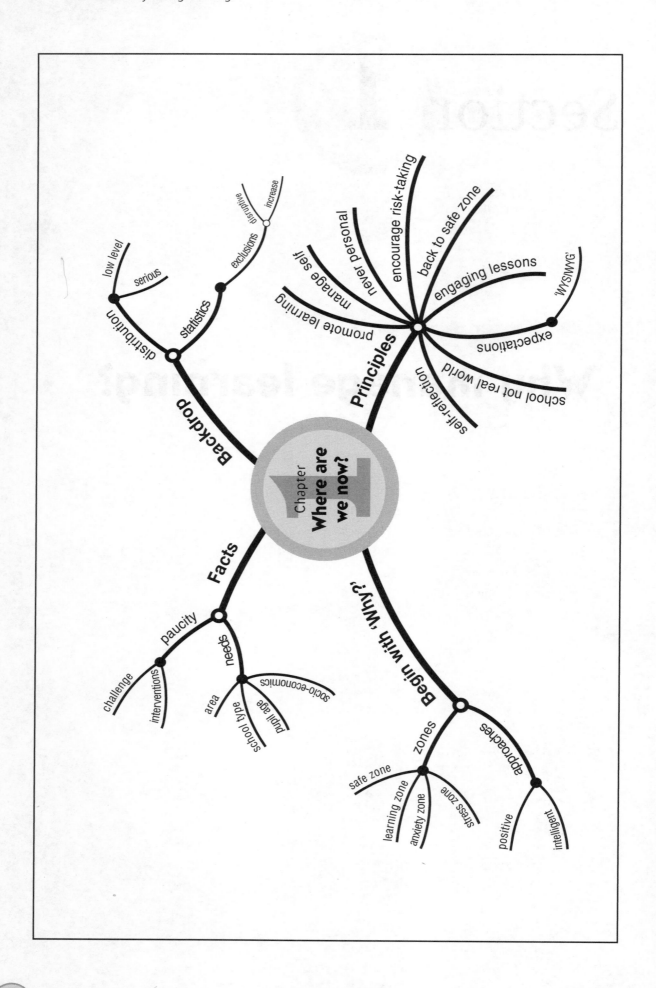

Chapter 1
**Where are we now?**

Backdrop
- distribution
  - serious
  - low level
  - statistics
    - exclusions
      - disruptive
      - increase

Principles
- promote learning
- manage self
- never personal
- encourage risk-taking
- back to safe zone
- engaging lessons
- 'WYSIWYG'
- expectations
- school not real world
- self-reflection

Facts
- paucity
  - challenge
  - interventions
  - needs
    - area
    - school type
    - pupil age
    - socio-economics

Begin with 'Why?'
- zones
  - safe zone
  - learning zone
  - anxiety zone
  - stress zone
- approaches
  - positive
  - intelligent

Challenging Behaviour – **A fresh look at promoting positive learning behaviours**

# Chapter 1

# Where are we now?

'Children today are tyrants. They contradict their parents, gobble their food and tyrannize their teachers.'

(Leading teacher)

## In this chapter you will:

- gain an overview of the contents of the book.
- acquire some of the statistical data associated with the current state of behaviour in UK schools.
- discover the principles of effective behaviour management.

## Preview questions

- What are the principles that you are currently operating on in school, in relation to behaviour management?
- How real is the behaviour problem that is highlighted in the press?
- What is currently working well for you in relation to behaviour management?
- What are your challenges and what would you like as alternatives?

# Where are we now?

So it is official, children are now more difficult to handle in schools. If the scant statistics are to be believed, then there is an increase in the incidence of unruly behaviour in our schools. David Bell, quoted by the Secondary Heads Association, said 'Ofsted's report on behaviour in schools [March 2005] revealed "worrying" numbers of disruptive and unruly pupils, but [David Bell] added that strong leadership and good teaching could turn the figures around'.

# Anecdotes and statistics

There would seem to be much anecdotal evidence around to support this assertion, and a hot topic of conversation in staffrooms all around the country is the latest misdemeanours of the youth of today. But how new is this? Is it really on the increase, or are we the victims of a press-perception-manipulation? Is it low-level disruption or the more serious violent criminal acts in schools that are most concerning? Teachers in schools would probably say both. One threatens the personal safety and security of dedicated teachers, not to mention their physical and mental health; the other potentially threatens the one chance that young people have to prepare themselves for the realities of life beyond school. The much-championed Elton Report in 1989 suggested that schools that provided consistent behaviour policies and good systems of pastoral care, and placed value on home–school relationships, were more effective in promoting good work and behaviour. It concluded that schools had an important role to play in reducing the risk of children becoming violent.

Figures on school exclusions released in 2005 show that heads are taking action and permanently excluding pupils where their behaviour is unacceptable. Exclusions were up by 6 per cent in 2003/4 on the previous year. Data published for the first time on the reasons for exclusion shows that persistent disruptive behaviour accounted for 30 per cent of all exclusions; verbal abuse and threatening behaviour against an adult accounted for 20 per cent; and assault against a pupil accounted for 20 per cent. It does appear in this report that exclusions are still lower by 20 per cent than the all-time recorded high of 12,668 exclusions in 1996/97.

# Fact or fallacy?

But do these figures really tell us anything about the state of behaviour in schools? Probably not. Steve Sinnott, General Secretary of the National Union of Teachers, wrote to Tony Blair in May 2005. In his letter, he described 'the paucity of valuable statistical information on the issue of pupil behaviour generally and violence in schools in particular'. He went on to suggest that 'this lack [of statistics] makes it impossible to analyse data for underlying patterns linking the incidence of violence, for example, to type of area, type of school, pupil age, socio-economic factors and more'. This makes the issue muddy and, in terms of the intervention, difficult for government to act upon.

Times change, but change takes time, and this is especially true when there is legislation involved.

While you wait for more statistics and for electric cattle prods and rubber bullets to be legalized in the classroom, what can you do each Wednesday afternoon at 2.30pm when you have the class from hell? If you cannot wait for the machine of government to package and post you the statistics, let alone the latest lunch-pack of answers, here are some helpful tips and ideas to make a difference in your classroom, your department or your school.

## Managing behaviour: begin with the *Why?*

What follows in this book are sets of principles, models, advice and strategies to help you turn lions into learners. It is very important to begin by thinking about *why* students misbehave before we think about *how* we tackle it. Understanding the reasons why children behave inappropriately informs the approaches we can use to promote positive learning behaviour. An understanding of how our behaviour as teachers interacts and influences that of learners is essential if we are to build sustainable positive classrooms.

In this book, I refer to four behavioural zones in which students and teachers operate:

- The safe zone: where students feel a sense of safety, self-worth and physical and emotional security.

- The learning zone: where students are challenged but at the same time supported to learn.

- The anxiety zone: where students begin to experience negative stress about the learning experience, and low-level misbehaviour happens.

- The stress zone: where students react in the classroom, are violent or uncontrollably abusive.

These zones exist in a dynamic structure called the Learning Zone Model, which is referred to throughout the book to support an intelligent and positive approach to managing young people.

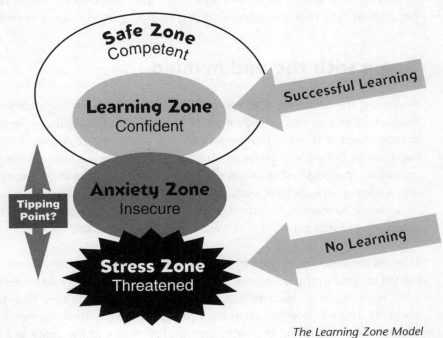

*The Learning Zone Model*

The Learning Zone Model provides a useful reference point to begin managing student behaviour. Similarly, it is a convenient tool for exploring our own behaviour as managers, teachers and teaching assistants and the influence this has on learners.

## Principles for encouraging learning behaviours

A series of principles underpin the Learning Zone Model. Adopting these principles will help you align with the mindset and beliefs that make the approaches in this book work. They are as follows.

1 Promote positive learning behaviours.
2 Manage your own learning behaviours in order to manage your students'.
3 It is never personal.
4 Encourage learners to take risk and support risk-taking.
5 Recognize that in a crisis, students need to go back to their safe zone before they can be in the learning zone again.
6 Children are more likely to behave if the lesson is engaging, varied and enjoyable: plan for it to be so.
7 Your expectations create your outcomes: focus on what you want, not what you do not want.
8 School is not the real world – take care not to take it too seriously.
9 Teacher self-reflection supports progress.

From time to time the situations we meet in school, challenge such principles. There may be occasions when principles are really tested. I would encourage you to stick with them. What is most important about principles is that they give you hope and direction when the going gets tough. By way of insight, you might like to give yourself a score out of ten for your adherence to each principle – make ten total adherence and one no adherence at all. Once you have scored this, consider in turn what the benefits might be of having each principle at ten. Then consider what you might need to change in order to achieve this.

## Begin with the end in mind

Reviewing the principles that you are operating on in your classroom provides useful insights. Principles can provide a set of ideals to aim for. With any approach to behaviour management, it is helpful to 'begin with the end in mind' (Covey 1989). Thinking about the kinds of behaviours you want in your classroom is a crucial starting point. It is important to decide what you want and to make sure that these expectations are keyed into learning expectations, with sound reasoning behind them. Your expectations need to make sense to learners for them to accept them and buy into them. There can be a tendency to focus on what is *not* wanted in the classroom.

There is an uncanny phenomenon called 'WYSIWYG' or 'what you see is what you get'. It relates to getting the outcomes that you fixate upon. Advanced drivers are familiar with what happens when they fix their attention on an obstacle they wish to avoid as they are skidding. There is a tendency to steer towards it, even if they do *not* want to hit it. If, on the other hand, they fix their attention on the road and the space available, they steer towards that and into safety. A similar principle operates in a classroom. If you focus on what you do not want, such as not calling out, not fighting and so on, then that is exactly what you will get. Instead, if you focus on hands up, waiting your turn and asking politely for resources, then that is what you will get. The complex processes that lead to this involve the way we represent our goals and how our unconscious mind processes and communicates negatives, as well as the interactions we have with others. Similarly, our language structure has an impact. The part of our mind that picks up on motivators in language has a curious way of processing negatives such as 'do not talk'. Before it can process the negative 'do not', it must first form a representation of the action it is not supposed to do, as if it were doing it. Therefore, the recipient of the request 'do not talk' first forms a picture of themselves talking and then (if you are lucky) processes the negative. Many students only get as far as processing the 'talk' part.

Being absolutely clear about what you expect, couched in the positive language of what you want, is essential. The behaviour in UK schools may well be shifting and also being amplified by perception. The paradox of flexibility with consistency will bring positive results for teachers. Coupling a consistent set of shared expectations with the flexible use of strategies makes a difference. Teachers have always needed that flexibility and, to date, it is this flexibility that has enabled them to respond to the educational changes over the last two decades.

There is nothing more constant than change, but the leading teacher quoted at the beginning of this chapter as saying 'Children today are tyrants. They contradict their parents, gobble their food and tyrannize their teachers' was in fact Socrates (469–399BC).

## Summary

- There is some evidence that disruptive behaviour in schools in England is on the rise. A lack of valuable statistical information makes it difficult to analyse trends and patterns in this area.

- There is growing anecdotal evidence from press cuttings, news reports and the conversations with colleagues about shifts in the attitudes of young people towards learning.

- This book outlines a series of simple principles, models, advice and strategies for managing student behaviour.

- There are four behavioural zones and the book details the dynamic between them.

- There are nine key principles for encouraging positive learner behaviours.

## Self-coaching insight questions

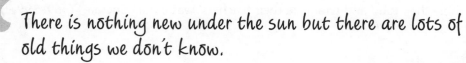

- What is the anecdotal evidence in your school for a shift in student behaviour?
- How accurate are the anecdotes?
- Looking at the principles outlined in the chapter:
  → Which principles do you operate on most of the time?
  → Which do you operate on some of the time?
  → Which would you like to operate on more of the time?
  → What could be the benefits of your operating on this latter principle more of the time?

❝ There is nothing new under the sun but there are lots of old things we don't know.

(Ambrose Bierce) ❞

❝ No one has yet realized the wealth of sympathy, the kindness and generosity hidden in the soul of a child. The effort of every true education should be to unlock that treasure.

(Emma Goldman) ❞

❝ And the day came when the risk to remain tight in a bud was more painful than the risk it took to blossom.

(Anais Nin) ❞

"There is nothing clever about not being happy.

(Arnauld Desjardins)

"We must especially learn the art of directing mindfulness into the closed areas of our life.

(Anais Nin)

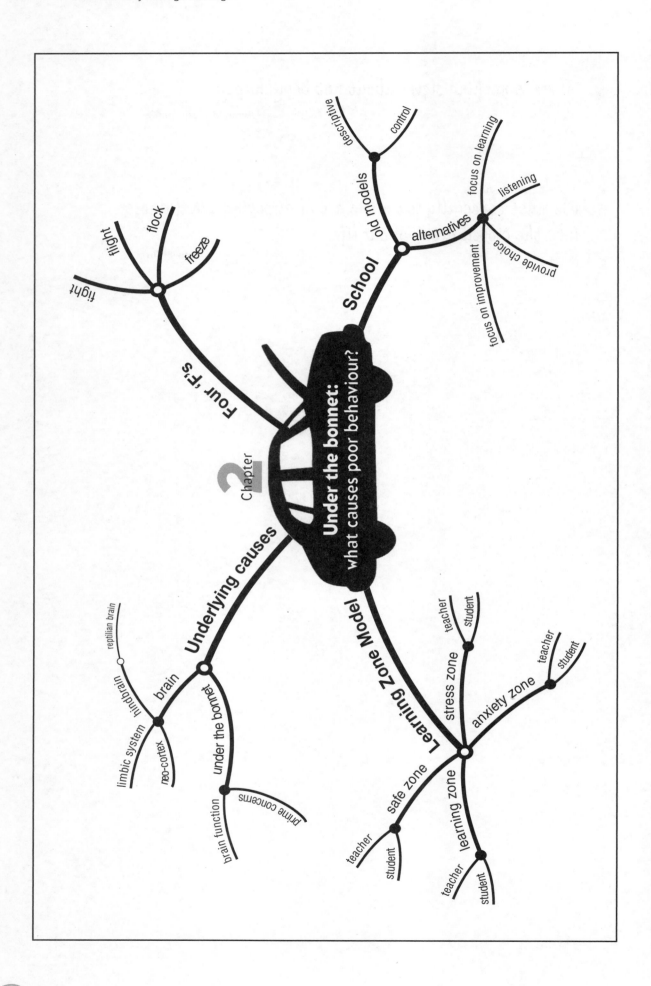

Challenging Behaviour – A fresh look at promoting positive learning behaviours

## Chapter 2

# Under the bonnet: what causes poor behaviour?

 *To find out how to fix a breakdown, start by looking under the bonnet.*

## In this chapter you will:

- gain crucial background into the way the learning zones improve learner behaviour.
- understand how knowing the inner workings of the brain will help you dramatically improve your ability to choose the most effective intervention strategy.
- understand the function of the hindbrain and the limbic system in response to stimuli.
- learn what children, adults and cars all have in common.

## Preview questions

- How will reading this book make even more sense of what you already know about managing behaviour?
- What is unique about this approach to managing behaviour?
- How might you save time, energy and emotional investment in managing your classroom, your students and your school?
- How might understanding more about the brain mean you build better relationships with your learners?

# Getting under the bonnet: an introduction to the brain

Few people can ignore the furore over the nature of student behaviour in schools. There may be, however, too much emphasis on the problem of behaviour and not enough on the underlying causes.

Arguably, the real purpose of teachers' work in schools is to create successful learners. Successful schools have a focus on learning. They are doing this through a genuine focus on the process of learning, the process of learners themselves and processes that work.

The inappropriate student behaviour that is reported in schools is often unique to the school environment. It is easy to forget that schools are not the 'real world', they are institutions often created with little reference to that 'real world'. It can be the case that many young people do very well beyond school and become successful adults despite their experience and apparent 'failure' at school.

The list of 'successful' people who were deemed difficult or challenging in academic life includes Winston Churchill, Albert Einstein and Robbie Williams. Consequently, perhaps, there is more to learn about the channelling of talent and the nature of success.

There is an argument therefore for examining and changing the factors, the cultures, the motivators and the approaches that influence behaviour. This focus puts the emphasis on changing the culture of the school rather than changing the young person. The problems and the answers do not lie only within the student, but also within the structures, behaviours and culture of the school. Despite challenging circumstances, there are many great examples around of successful teachers, schools and learners.

## Case Study

Wild Bank Primary School is a 130-place school in a run-down area of Tameside, Greater Manchester.

### Background

The class is a mixture of Year 1 and 2 who had a history of low achievement and poor behaviour in Reception. Their proposed class teacher for the autumn term 2005 was on maternity leave until February 2006 and another teacher was employed from late June 2005 to provide temporary cover. She became the full-time teacher of the class in September 2005.

This teacher's initial observations confirmed that many pupils had special needs and most were underachieving. Their general behaviour was poor and some could be challenging and difficult. Many of the pupils were experiencing difficulties in their home lives; some had already been referred to social services.

Assessments confirmed that the vast majority of pupils were 18 months to 2 years behind on their expected progress and they had not established the basic behaviours needed to participate in learning.

The teacher used the principles of managing behaviour and the Learning Zone Model to plan and carry out the following activities. She began by establishing a very clear 'safe zone' and then structured the 'learning zone'.

## Her approach

Wild Bank is an open-plan school and the environment itself presented challenges. The classroom is a strange shape and leads into the next class. The original carpeted gathering area was too small for the 28 pupils to congregate and had the corridor running through it. The room was far too busy for pupils who needed calm and structure in their classroom.

The classroom had to be reorganized to provide the 'safe zone' with the calm, ordered routines that young children need. The interactive whiteboard needed to be accommodated and so the carpet area was moved to create an area with far fewer distractions. Free-standing display boards were commandeered to provide the new 'learning zone'; there was a deliberate renaming of the carpet area that had previously been associated with poor behaviour rather than learning. The rest of the display areas were made into 'displays for learning' and the whole classroom was much more orderly and distraction free. Pupils' learning groups were renamed and given clear parameters.

The physical environment was thus reorganized to take into account the need for clear boundaries and designated distraction-free learning zones. The provision of this structure and clear physical boundaries immediately reduced the high levels of anxiety previously displayed by the pupils.

A series of regimented physical routines were implemented. For example, entry into the classroom, hanging up of book bags and coats was taught, reinforced with praise and had a sense of fun attached. Digressions were at first dealt with in a zero-tolerance fashion, and soon became unusual and could be dealt with through humour or cajoling.

This approach moved pupils towards greater independence. The teacher established clear positive expectations of behaviour and shifted class expectations from prior labels of 'wild' and 'low in ability' to 'resourceful' and 'untapped potential'. She established clear targets for the class for the end of the year. She then fine-tuned that to what would be the focus each week.

$\rightarrow$

## Teacher actions

Below are some of the actions the teacher took.

### Proactive classroom structures:

- 👍 A well defined learning zone, comfortable and free from distractions, and positioned away from 'traffic'.
- 👍 Clear, fun, 'stop signals' and rewards for stopping during fun activities.
- 👍 Carefully split activities with lots of time out to fidget.
- 👍 Shorter spells of sitting.
- 👍 Use of puppets and other novelty events to engage pupils.

### Reactive interventions:

- 👍 Structured, deliberate use of praise for getting things right, including reward systems.
- 👍 Lots of low key, teacher interventions, that is, the teacher's use of non-verbal signals.
- 👍 Low key praise, such as a wink or a thumbs up, when the right behaviour occurs.

In addition, she also looked carefully at ways to promote a more positive response to learning from a group of young children who had already established a poor picture of themselves as learners. Therefore she planned the learning with emphasis on 'how' the children were going to learn rather than just 'what'. Emphasis was placed on genuine differentiation to take into account the children's attitudes to learning as well as ability levels. Learning had to be well structured and fun. Much use was made of opportunities to divide learning into bite-size pieces with recognition of the different ways of learning, including VAK.

## Progress

Reassessment of levels of learning established that the vast majority of pupils have progressed significantly. Other evidence of success included:

- 👍 the class are no longer being referred to as the 'wild bunch' in school by staff.
- 👍 the class achieving an accolade for their first class-assembly.
- 👍 the class teacher very rarely having to use second-line behaviour tactics, that is, it is rare for children to be sent to the headteacher on discipline matters.
- 👍 the children on individual programmes having evidence of progress and parents commenting on how much happier and better behaved their children were at home.

Within this encouraging case study, there is both strategy and hope. Having high expectations of pupils and adopting a zero-tolerance approach to promoting the highest quality learning behaviour works. We can have control without being controlling. It is possible to facilitate excellence without inciting conflict.

# The mind and the art of vehicle maintenance

One of the reasons why many behaviour management approaches do not appear to work is because they fail to address the underlying reasons why learners misbehave. For strategies to be effective, they must be appropriate to the circumstances. Picking the appropriate strategy for the group, child or behaviour relies upon having an understanding of the workings of the individual or collective mind.

A useful analogy here is that of the mechanical breakdown of your car. If you are only offered the tools to fix it, it would be difficult to know where to begin. With more understanding of the mechanics of the car, you can begin to use the tools correctly and in the right part of the car. Without proper knowledge of the workings of the car, there is the risk that we will cause greater harm. An understanding of what is going on under the bonnet is equally important in the management of young people.

# The brain and behaviour

Having some awareness of the brain's structure and function can be beneficial in understanding and selecting the most appropriate behaviour management tools to use in the classroom. The intention here is to keep it as simple as possible and no simpler.

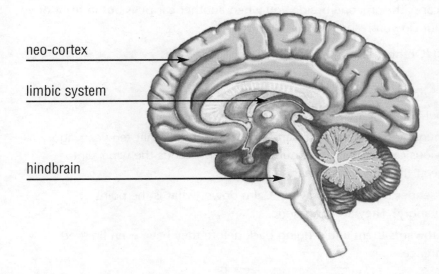

The brain is an immensely complex organ. Indeed, experts do not all agree on the exact structural and functional relationships within it. There is a huge variation between people's brains and thus what is offered here is a generalized model.

The brain is made up of a vast collection of specialized nerve cells called neurones and supportive cells. It can broadly be divided into three key parts:

● neo-cortex
● limbic system
● hindbrain or reptilian brain.

The neo-cortex consists of the frontal lobe, the parietal lobe, the temporal lobe and the occipital lobe. The frontal lobe deals with long-term planning and understanding the consequences of our actions. The parietal lobe deals with speaking and sense of touch. The temporal lobe handles hearing and smell with some memory function and the occipital lobe houses our visual processing function. The limbic system consists of the amygdala, hippocampus and thalamus. It houses long-term memory and deals with short cuts when coping with danger. The limbic system is also the emotional centre of the brain and acts as a gatekeeper, sending stimuli to appropriate parts of the brain. The hindbrain or reptilian brain deals with strictly survival issues. It is an instinctive structure that regulates breathing, blood sugar and other physiological levels. It also mediates the survival behaviours of fight, flight, flock and freeze (the so-called four 'F's) (Sapolsky 1998).

What is important in terms of considering classroom behaviour is the relationships between the three areas. The neo-cortex manages higher level thinking, whereas the limbic system has an emotional function. The hindbrain deals with instinctive survival processes. Stimuli do not enter the brain via the neo-cortex, but through the limbic system. Consequently, the distribution of data entering the brain is managed through an emotional gateway. When stimuli enter the amygdala in the limbic system they are channelled to other areas. If they are considered to be threatening stimuli, they are channelled quickly to the hindbrain. The neo-cortex catches up later. What you get then is a response that lacks rational processing. It is an emergency response.

By way of illustration of this in action, consider your responses as a car driver. Imagine you are driving in your car with someone beside you when another car pulls out in front of you, narrowly missing you. Do you respond by:

a) Calmly saying 'Oh how terribly vexing...'

Or

b) Shouting out angrily 'You idiot...' and so on.

   (i)   Using foul language that you would never normally use.

   (ii)  Simultaneously slamming your hand on a control stalk that ten years ago in a previous car was the horn, but now viciously sends the wipers into overdrive at the now long departed 'idiot'.

   (iii) Your passenger turning and saying 'Calm down, what is the point of being so angry? They are long gone.'

   (iv)  Turning towards them and arguing back before they have even finished their sentence.

Perhaps option b, or a lesser version of it, is the more likely scenario. Although this situation may not be a trigger (our so-called 'hot button') for everyone, it is likely that you can relate to it or something similar.

## So what's happening in your brain at this point?

Certain triggers cause the limbic system to rapidly transmit data to the hindbrain and an auto-response system occurs. When the hindbrain is alerted, we revert to the primitive behaviours associated with survival. These behaviours have little to do with considered rational thinking and much to do with aggression, escape and safety.

The behaviours we exhibit at times of stress can be categorized as 'the four 'F's'.

- **FIGHT** – stand up and physically or verbally resist
- **FLIGHT** – run away from the stimulus, or divert attention away from the risk
- **FLOCK** – stick together as a herd – safety in numbers
- **FREEZE** – like a rabbit in the headlights, cease to function.

In the scene in the car, you, as the driver, see the other car and this triggers fear that leads to unconscious survival behaviours that leave you unable to consider other more thoughtful behaviour.

Your passenger, on the other hand, is less threatened and is capable of seeing more clearly and responding with their neo-cortex. In managing behaviour effectively in the classroom, teachers must develop the ability to be a driver and a passenger and create meaningful dialogue between the two. Survival behaviours are learned and can be unlearned.

## The brain in school

The same sort of process described above is also seen in classrooms. A teacher and student can respond to one another in a way that triggers reptilian brain responses in each. The result can be an escalating and highly emotional exchange from both parties. Neither means to respond in this way, yet both do.

Consider this situation: a student has completed a series of maths problems. She has come to the front of the class to have them marked. She scores 0 out of 10 as all the sums have incorrect answers. The following dialogue outlines what might occur in a classroom setting.

| | |
|---|---|
| **Teacher** | OK, you've had some difficulties with this. Let's look at where you can make this better next time. *(teacher being positive and encouraging)* |
| **Student** | I don't want to! I've already spent loads of time on it. *(student experiencing feeling of threat internally and responds sharply)* |
| **Teacher** | *(tone of voice that student has used has triggered an incensed feeling in the teacher)* Yes and so have I! We spent hours going over how to do this ... you'll have to stay in at break and do it all again. *(response has escalated)* |
| **Student** | I've already spent loads of time on it. I'm not staying in. *(student has escalated in response to withdrawal of freedom)* |
| **Teacher** | You obviously aren't listening to my teaching – it's time you realized that school is not just for you to meet your mates ... you need to focus ... it's quite typical of you. *(now the teacher is moving to make generalized statements about the student that further threaten her self-esteem)* |
| **Student** | What's the point of talking to you, you never listen ... I'm not staying in and you can't make me. |
| **Teacher** | If I decide you're staying in, you will and you will...' *(a variety of aggressive body language is also exhibited by both parties, the teacher pointing a finger at the student)* |

When our emotional responses, such as fear or defiance, are activated, our reptilian brain engages. Triggered in us are learned behaviours that we experienced in similar situations when we were young. These default survival behaviours are often based on past models of discipline and control from our own parents or teachers. Our beliefs and fears associated with threats to our authority, security or expectations, turn the rational into personalized and inappropriate approaches.

Here are some key points about areas of error and improvement for our teacher above:

1   Error – drawing a conclusion that the child was not listening. Instead, the teacher should explore reasons why the child did not understand.

2   Error – escalating the situation to a sanction. Instead, maintain a focus on how the learning could be improved.

3   Error – focusing on deficit behaviour (that is, not listening). Instead, focus on the specific things the child could do to improve their score.

4   Error – making unenforceable ultimatums. This student, like many others, values freedom, so in an already emotionally charged situation the sanction of staying in is likely to heighten feelings further. Instead, if sanctions are appropriate, offer choice or, at worst, the illusion of choice in order to avoid flat refusal to comply.

This teacher also needs to be aware of their own 'prime concerns'. Prime concerns are unresolved issues at a deep, unconscious level. They surface usually when they are triggered by another person saying specific words (often in connection with a specific intonation) and bring about an irrational and inappropriate response. Most of us have prime concerns. Through becoming aware of them, and through experience, we can begin to understand which words, voice tones and associated body language trigger inappropriate responses in us. Understanding these physical, auditory and visual triggers allows us to maintain better neo-cortical control.

The problem with ignoring these prime concerns and the behaviours they trigger is that we can end up modelling the behaviour to our students that we want them to stop doing.

To allow us to raise our awareness of these triggers we use a simple and effective four-part behaviour model.

# The Learning Zone Model – how to stay in control

It would seem that making schools stress-free places, where teachers always respond calmly and thoughtfully, is the route to better-behaved students. In a sense, this is absolutely right; however, it is easier said than done. We are, after all, dealing with human beings and we actually need some stress in order to perform at our best, both as learners and as teachers.

For learning to take place, we require 'an environment of high challenge and low stress' (Smith and Call 1999). If learners are to learn, they do need to move from a safe zone of no stress and no challenge to a stretch zone where there is challenge and a small amount of helpful, so-called 'green stress' (Thomas 2005). What we must avoid is learners moving into a zone of negative stress where 'red stress' exists. Red stress is the stress that can trigger unpredictable behaviours, including verbal and even physical violence towards self and others.

*The Learning Zone Model*

When we are safe and unchallenged, we are not learning. Learning itself requires an element of risk-taking and challenge; but when does challenge become stress? The Learning Zone Model helps us to understand this.

Let us revisit the four behavioural zones in which both students and teachers operate:

- The safe zone: where students feel a sense of safety, self-worth and physical and emotional security. This promotes the conditions to be able to take on the challenge of learning.

- The learning zone: where students are challenged but at the same time supported to learn. This is a zone of high challenge and low negative stress.

- The anxiety zone: where students begin to experience negative stress about the learning experience, and low-level misbehaviour happens. This can be because the challenge is too high and does not have sufficient scaffolding to allow learners to make sufficiently small steps towards mastery. It can sometimes be because the challenge is too low and children are bored. It is also where they will be if the safe zone is not first established.

- The stress zone: where students react in the classroom, are violent or uncontrollably abusive. This is the zone from which there is no easy route back to the learning zone. It is a zone of crisis for the student.

The vast majority of misbehaviour in schools takes place in the anxiety zone. The good news is that students can be nurtured back into the learning zone from here. The stress zone is, however, the 'point of no return'. Behaviours that are extreme and a long way from learning require specific skills in de-escalating conflict and returning students to the safe zone. Only then can they be supported to return to the challenge of the learning zone. Attempts to move students from the stress zone directly to the learning zone result in escalation of conflict.

In the remainder of the book, the Learning Zone Model is used as a framework for understanding and responding to the behavioural responses of young people.

## Summary

- Inappropriate student behaviour is a significant issue in many UK schools.
- A focus on behaviour rather than on learning may be the cause of limited success with strategies for managing behaviour.
- Schools represent an artificial environment from which learners may graduate unsuccessfully, yet go on to be great successes beyond compulsory education.
- Behaviour problems are far more likely to be solved through a focus on learning rather than a focus on behaviour.
- The brain has a reptilian system that is wired up for survival. The reptilian system generates survival behaviours at times of anxiety/stress.
- Survival behaviours can be referred to as the 'four 'F's'.
- The degree to which we tip into survival behaviour affects the degree to which we are rational in our response to stimuli.
- Student behaviour is only half the story. How adults respond to student behaviour influences the escalation of inappropriate behaviour or the promotion of learning behaviour.

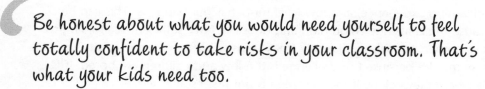

Be honest about what you would need yourself to feel totally confident to take risks in your classroom. That's what your kids need too.

(Will Thomas)

When the going gets tough, you need to know where home is.

(Anon)

Advice is what we ask for when we already know the answer but wish we didn't.

(Erica Jong)

# Self-coaching insight questions

If you can discuss your responses to these questions with someone else, you may gain additional insight. Encourage any partner you work with to ask open questions – that is, what, when, where, who – to deepen your insights.

1   Think of a time when a student over-stepped the mark and you felt you responded well.
     → How did you react?
     → What were the features of that successful reaction?
     → What state of mind were you in prior to this situation?
     → How did you know that the response was appropriate?

2   Think of a time when a student over-stepped the mark and you felt that you responded less appropriately.
     → How did you react?
     → What were the features of that less successful reaction?
     → What state of mind were you in prior to this situation?
     → How did you know that your response was less appropriate?

3   Now compare the two situations.
     → What are the differences?
     → What are you learning here?

4   What were your experiences as a child in school?

5   What is important to you in relation to children's behaviour in school?

6   In the answers to questions 4 and 5 above
     → What helps you in the classroom now?
     → What hinders you in the classroom now?

# Section 2

## What creates learning behaviour?

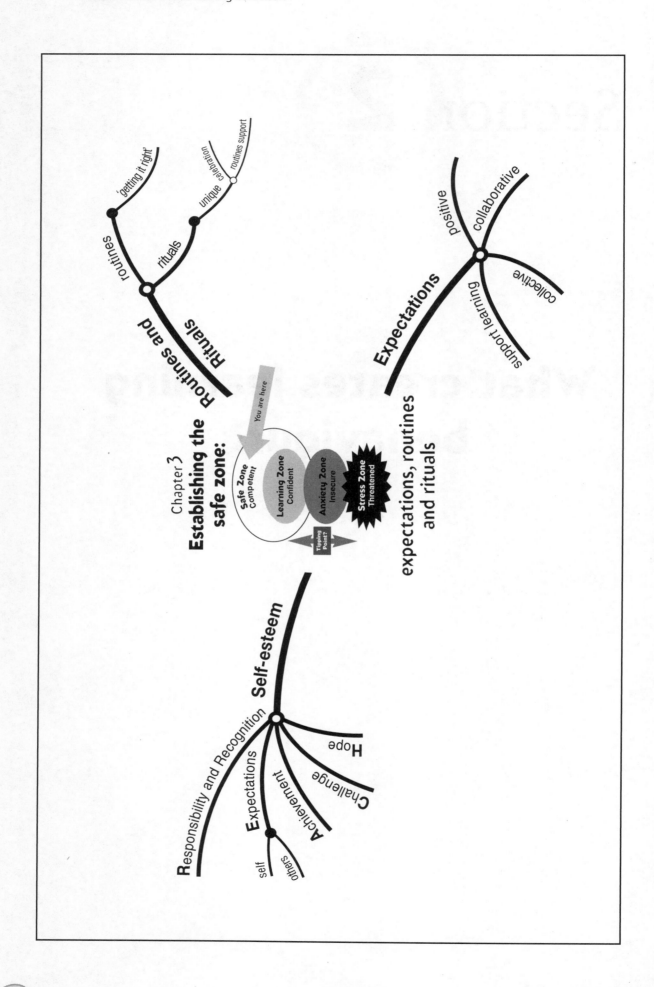

Chapter 3

**Establishing the safe zone:**

**Routines and Rituals**

expectations, routines and rituals

**Chapter 3**

# Establishing the safe zone: expectations, routines and rituals

*We tried to set up an anarchic society but no one would agree to the rules and regulations.*

## In this chapter you will:

- further understand the importance of learner self-esteem in effective classrooms.
- meet the REACH approach to building and maintaining self-esteem.
- understand the relationship between rules and expectations.
- know the difference between routines and rituals and have strategies for the implantation of each.

## Preview questions

- How is self-esteem currently playing a role in learning in your classroom or school? How are you currently managing this dynamic?
- What are the expectations in your school or classroom?
- How are they arrived at?
- Who plays a part in the development of expectations?

# Playing safe

In this chapter, we explore the safe zone of the Learning Zone Model. We will look at what needs to be established in your school or classroom so that there is a consistent foundation to enable learners to rise to the challenge of learning. The same foundation ensures that they have a place to retreat to should they move into high-level stress states.

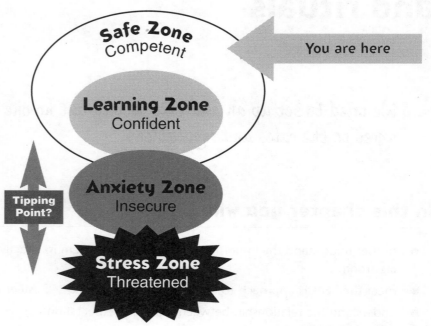

*The Learning Zone Model*

There are essentially two areas that need to be addressed in establishing the safe zone:

1    The emotional safety of learners – through a framework known as REACH.
2    The physical and process safety – through routines and rituals.

It is argued in Chapter 2 that positive effective learning can take place only when we feel emotionally and physically safe and secure, that is, when we feel confident to take the risks, possessing the positive self-esteem needed to be successful in the learning state.

To this end the foundation of all learning has to be the establishment and maintenance of high self-esteem for all our students, and a high degree of predictability about the processes by which schools operate.

# Establishing emotional security in the safe zone

Within the safe zone, there are a series of key elements that are essential to students for building and maintaining positive self-esteem, which is a strong sign of emotional security. Self-esteem is the interplay between our own self-image and the expectations placed upon us by ourselves and others. If we have a poor self-image and there are conversely high expectations upon us, our self-esteem will be low. On the other hand, if we have high self-image and appropriately high expectations placed upon us, then our self-esteem is high. In the latter situation, we feel emotionally secure and more willing to take risks. Self-esteem is highly contextualized and it is necessary to provide constants that enable students to feel sure about their emotional environment.

These constants are conveniently summarized within the REACH framework shown below. REACH is the promotion of positive:

**R**esponsibility and **R**ecognition

**E**xpectations of self and others

**A**chievement

**C**hallenge

**H**ope

## What the REACH framework means

Below is an elaboration of the REACH framework for establishing a safe zone in classrooms.

**R** Responsibility is the promotion and celebration of every individual taking responsibility for themselves and others. Recognition is about positively recognizing and celebrating the achievements of all students whatever their talent.

**E** Expectation is about how you promote and support high expectations of individuals and their expectations of others.

**A** Achievement is how much do you/the school celebrate all forms of achievement by every student.

**C** Challenge is making sure that challenge is promoted for each individual and that risk-taking is supported to meet the needs of different students.

**H** Hope is about providing new, fresh hope and aspirations for the generations of young people and adults who have lost sight of any hope!

To understand this in practice, we might consider two students: one shows high levels of self-esteem and the other, lower levels.

John    is often placed in positions of *responsibility*. He is captain of his form football team and regularly gains lots of positive *recognition* from both students and adults for this.

John    has realistic yet high *expectations* and he uses positive language (speaking out) and positive self-talk (inner voice) to describe himself and his experiences.

| | |
|---|---|
| John | *achieves* in many different aspects of school life, academically and in extra-curricular, and is popular with his peers. |
| John | is suitably *challenged* and enjoys having a go at new things. |
| John | has many plans for his future and is forward thinking. His *hopes* are challenging and are supported by his family. |
| Sophie | could not be trusted to take on even a minor *responsibility*. She is *recognized* in school, but for all the wrong reasons. She is actually a very good athlete but no one knows that in school. |
| Sophie | comes from a family where neither parents nor grandparents have jobs and she *expects* to go on to benefits when she leaves school. |
| Sophie | sees herself as a waster and frequently thinks and says 'What's the point? This is boring.' Her reports are littered with comments about under *achievement*. |
| Sophie | frequently challenges authority but avoids any *challenge* in her schoolwork and most teachers expect very little of her. |
| Sophie | For Sophie, quite simply, what is *hope*? |

Building and maintaining self-esteem has a great deal to do with the day-to-day beliefs and expectations children experience in their classroom from their teachers, teaching assistants and peers. The REACH model provides a useful way to audit success of our safe zone. By breaking the safe zone down into the five parts of REACH, we can more specifically address the needs of the individual (or group). Consider analysing your group or an individual student using the REACH framework. For each aspect, consider the question: How am I currently supporting the establishment of this? There are more strategies on how to create a more emotionally safe and supportive environment in Section 3.

In many ways, the expectations provide the most critical aspect of establishing an emotionally safe environment within the REACH model. To this end, the expectations element of REACH requires further elaboration.

## Expectations

Expectations need to be established. Creating expectations needs to be the collective responsibility of those expected to comply with them. A strong sense of collaboration is required to ensure that expectations become a reality. These should always support learning and not simply be about inflicting conformity. In other words, expectations are about making learning easier, not about 'toeing the line'. Where expectations are established but do not support learning, they will be challenged and broken, especially by older students.

Expectations reflect the willingness to accept that there is a need to work together rather than challenge and confront. We are not able to control, merely to influence; and many of our students live in homes with few, if any, boundaries and are no longer fearful or respectful of authority. We need to have expectations that support the core purpose of education – that of enabling learning.

Finally, expectations should always be presented in the positive. The focus on traditional rules in schools has tended to be more about what happens when you break the rules rather than what happens when you get them right. Our focus in the classroom needs to be about celebrating success and so we need to avoid negative rules, such as do not run in the corridor, do not call out, do not chew gum and so on.

We get more of what we reinforce in others, and having a strong focus on what not to do only highlights that as a behaviour. Similarly, it does nothing to present the positive behaviours that we are seeking to promote. On a psychological level, the unconscious part of a child's mind focuses on the command in the sentence, the part after the 'DO NOT'. Consequently, children are processing phrases such 'run in the corridor', 'call out' and 'chew gum', which reinforces the behaviour you wish to avoid. For many children, their unconscious mind does not make it back to the negation 'Do not', and so the rule becomes a command to carry out the forbidden behaviour!

It is also the case that if students can gain a lot of teacher attention with negative behaviour, then we are reinforcing that negative behaviour. We can, therefore, achieve considerably enhanced behaviour simply by being clear about what we would like to see and rewarding it when it appears. Remember:

> If you have a list of 'DO NOT …' on your classroom wall, you are advertising what you don't want!

The provision of clear, consistent boundaries gives us all a sense of security from which we are able to explore risk-taking. Without these clear boundaries, risk-taking is avoided or extreme. We live in an era where for some parents it seems easier to allow their children to find their own way completely rather than develop and explain boundaries. Where parenting is judged by what material rewards you provide for your children, rather than your ability to offer clear, concise supportive boundaries, problems can arise. The sense of security that such boundaries offer is essential in our growth towards adulthood. The good news is that this is highly contextualized and in school, in class and even in a one to one, you can create boundaries with young people and they will work to them; it is actually what they crave.

## Routines and rituals

The safe zone is not transitional, but a constant to which we return in times of particular anxiety or stress. The REACH model gives some insight into the emotional needs of students. As part of the establishment of a safe zone in the classroom and institution, there is also the need for security of process. This comes from the establishment of routines and rituals.

A definition of these would be:

- Routines support 'getting it right'.
- Rituals are the unique ways that support the routines and are about celebrating getting it right.

The expectations we explored within the REACH model form the boundaries of what is 'right'. So routines and rituals are used to support the adherence to those expectations.

## Routines

Routines are about providing the structure to support 'getting it right'. Routines are a crucial element of scaffolding for the learning journey. They offer an opportunity to make the journey more bearable and safe, balancing risk and adventure with a foundation of security.

Let us take a few moments to look at this in your context. Consider these questions.

- Do you have students who are anxious to know what time break is the moment they arrive in the morning?
- Do you have students who are thrown into anxiety by the merest change in their timetable?
- What about you? How do you feel if the layout of your room is disturbed or equipment is out of place?
- How often have you witnessed some unexpected and challenging responses to changes in routine from students or from colleagues?

The limbic brain that we met in Chapter 2 can be emotionally upset by simple changes to routines. The responses to the questions above may well provide personal evidence of this.

Without routines, students often choose not to try new ways of doing things in order to avoid the risk of getting things wrong. With routines in place, students feel more able to take a gamble, knowing they have a fall-back position, somewhere safe to return. On the simplest level, this can mean they trust that their teacher lives by the routine that if something does not work out as expected, they can decide what they learned from it and try again – a basic routine for learning.

Simple, structured entrance into and exit out of our learning space make a difference too. Routines that illustrate when and where learning begins and changes, such as task lines (a washing line across the room onto which cards with activities are pegged in the order they will happen), can help. Additionally, timetables and structured learning cycles (see, Smith et al. 2003) play an important part in the learning routine.

Paying attention to the detail of your learning environment and how easy or not it is to move around successfully is all part of establishing positive routines. Routines that support movement become essential in larger groups and institutions, especially where hundreds of students may need to move classes at any one time.

Routines do not just happen because you created an expectation. Routines need to be taught and modelled. This needs to be done in ways that emphasize their link with supporting learning.

So routines for processes, such as responding to mistakes, moving around the classroom, collecting resources or preparing for break times, need to be introduced, taught, modelled and rewarded when done correctly. When in place, they support the safe zone foundation of our lessons.

# Rituals

Rituals introduce uniqueness and fun; they promote a sense of belonging. Rituals should focus around positive emotions and how these aid learning. Rituals often provide subliminal reinforcement; for example, soothing music to promote calmness after the routine break time and occasional conflict between students. Similarly, they can be used to celebrate success with actions, songs and music; for example, a reward ceremony ritual for successful learning outcomes–: 'one hand up, two hands up, bring them together, give yourself a clap!'

Many teachers invent games to go with routines, such as movement down the corridor with KS1 walking like soldiers with songs and so on. These can be adjusted according to the age group you teach and are often triggered by the personality of the group concerned. Rituals invite imagination and fun and they positively market or sell routines and expectations.

Further examples of rituals and routines to establishing the safe zone in school could include:

- Students are met at the school entrance by the head and welcomed each morning.
- SMT in corridors to celebrate good behaviours and spot any potential difficulties.
- Teachers smiling and welcoming students as they enter the classroom.
- Getting started rituals such as 'Early Bird' work on desks.
- An agreed school or class learning cycle that is consistently applied, that is, it is what will happen in every lesson. For example, we will connect to what we know, then learn something new, then show each other what we have learned, then summarize what we have learned (see Smith et al. 2003).
- Routines for general learning and personal needs such as access to toilets or drinking water are needed. For example, wait for a time when the teacher is aware, then put up your hand. One school in the North East of England carefully selected music and inventive stop signals to manage time on tasks.

Teaching learners how to create their own learning routines and rituals reinforces their ability to become successful learners too. Allowing learners to be involved in the development of rituals allows them to be inventive and create responsible attitudes to keeping to expectations for themselves.

## Summary

- Offering poor or restricted learning opportunities only reinforces low expectations and low self-esteem. This can lead to unrest in its tendency to patronize students who are often quite capable.

- Learner self-esteem needs active management on a daily basis. REACH can provide a framework for auditing and troubleshooting issues relating to self-esteem.

- Our clear, learning-focused expectations ensure that learning can happen. They should be about what it looks like when learners get it right.

- Routines are about providing the structure to support getting it right. They need to be taught and modelled.

- Rituals add an element of fun and belonging to the expectations and routines we establish for learning. They are associated with positive emotions, such as calmness or success.

## Self-coaching insight questions

- On a scale of one to ten, where ten is high and one is low, how would you rate your awareness of the self-esteem of each of the learners in your class(es)?

- How could you use REACH to better understand the individual students or groups you teach?

- In your classroom or school, what are:
  → the rules
  → the expectations
  → the routines?
  → the rituals?

- What might need to change as a result of your being even more aware of the routines and rituals in your learning evironment?

" The direction in which education starts a man will determine his future life.

(Plato) "

" You always pass failure on the way to success.

(Mickey Rooney) "

" Success is the ability to go from one failure to another with no loss of enthusiasm.

(Winston Churchill) "

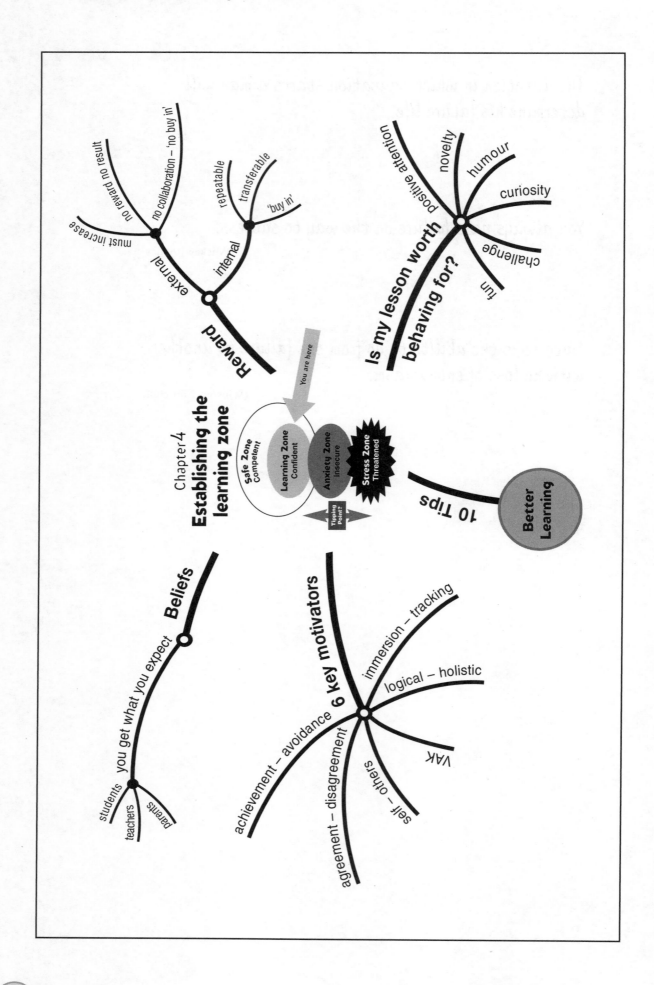

# Chapter 4
# Establishing the learning zone

> *Take care of the learning and the behaviour will take care of itself.*

## In this chapter you will:

- learn about how our expectations for good or bad can shape our outcomes.
- understand the principles of building an effective learning zone.
- be able to reflect upon the learning opportunities you provide in your classroom.

## Preview questions

- How do expectations shape outcomes?
- What would you rank as the top motivators in the classroom?
- How does variety shape outcome?
- If you were a child in your best lesson last week and in your worst lesson last week, what would you be thinking while you are sat in each lesson?

# Punished by reward – the essentials of motivating learning

In Chapter 3, we learned about the safe zone. In this chapter, we unpack the learning zone. This is where effective learning takes place and, as outlined in Chapter 3, this learning zone can only be entered once a safe zone foundation is in place. Here we explore the principles for achieving and maintaining the learning zone. The learning zone requires that children are challenged to take risks in the classroom – to step out of their comfort zones and grow emotionally and intellectually. For this to happen, there needs to be motivation, self-esteem and carefully structured learning experiences that take account of differences in learning preference.

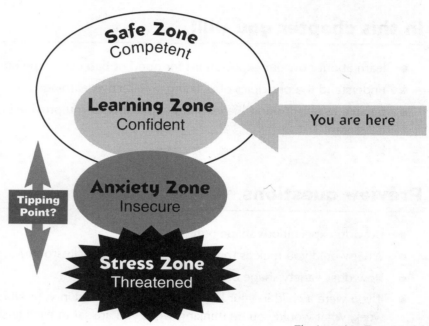

*The Learning Zone Model*

Kohn (2000) *Punished by Rewards* is an intriguing book that challenges some so-called 'positive behaviour management' perspectives. These perspectives encourage reward and, in some cases, promote an external reward culture. In this culture, children were encouraged to work towards external goals, such as stickers, pencil sharpeners and fast food vouchers. More recently we have begun to question this external motivation, as it seems that a number of unhelpful outcomes can occur:

1   Over time the external rewards have to increase in value (monetary and perceived value) for children to remain motivated by them.

2   When the physical reward is not there, there is often no internal motivation installed – in that sense, children are unable to self-motivate without the external reward.

3   Crucially these schemes are often set up without the involvement of the children themselves. Where they are imposed, they may not actually motivate at all.

Motivation is a fascinating and crucial area of classroom practice. In this chapter, we explore some of the key motivators that children have and how we can provide for them in the classroom.

# Exploring your own motivations first

In order to explore the nature of motivation in classrooms, it is helpful to consider our own motivation. In understanding ourselves, we can begin to understand both the motivations and the frustrations of those we teach.

Consider these questions:

- What truly makes you get up for work every day?
- Why did you choose the role you currently have?
- Where have you been happiest in your work in the past?
- What was it that caused you to choose to be happy then?
- Have you ever moved jobs despite receiving less pay? If yes, what was it that caused you to choose to do so?
- What's important to you in a job?
- What have you been learning about your motivations?

These sorts of questions may lead us to the conclusion that our own motivation stretches beyond tangible rewards such as pay, working hours and holidays. Value and rewards are highly individualized and what will excite for one, will not for another. The more we are personally investing in an outcome, the more motivated we are.

Part of my career was as a class teacher to a Year 10 group of boys in an EBD (Emotional and Behavioural Difficulties; nowadays referred to as EBSD – Emotional, Behavioural and Social Difficulties) boys' residential school – a challenging environment to work in. One day during a teaching session a student came up with a pretty smart idea.

| | |
|---|---|
| **Student** | Eh, miss we should have ace of the week! |
| **Me** | What do you mean? |
| **Student** | Well your initials are AC, add an E and we get ACE of the week. Top boy for the week. |
| **Other students** | Yeah, that's a good idea. |

*(By now I'm beginning to wonder if I'm being set up for some expensive, complicated reward scheme)*

| | |
|---|---|
| **First student** | Yeah, we all vote at the end of the week for who's worked hardest, and you have the final say. |
| **Me** | OK, but how much is it going to cost me? |
| **First student** | One pound. |

*(My thoughts: Am I being set up? What would one pound realistically buy these days? Why would these boys work extra hard for just one pound?)*

| | |
|---|---|
| **Me** | OK, but what if we can't decide who, or no one deserves it? |
| **First student** | We'll have a rollover. |

In short, we implemented this system and the reward scheme was highly successful and yet not thought of by me in any way. Let us examine why it was so productive.

First, it was owned by and respected by the participants, the students themselves, and agreed with by me as the teacher. The voting system and criteria were managed by the students, with me alongside. The prize at just one pound represented the essence of motivation. The money was not the true value of the reward, it was the recognition by people the students valued that mattered. The one pound was a token of that.

In designing your own reward systems, these guidelines could be helpful:

1   Make sure a reward has more intrinsic value than material value – in other words, the motivation for achieving the reward should focus on getting it right, not on what the students will get as a result.

2   Involve your students in defining the rewards wherever possible.

3   Be prepared to be flexible with the reward over time – once one area is working well, move the reward focus to another area and be willing to listen to your students again.

4   Be absolutely explicit in defining the criteria for achievement so as to maintain the integrity and value of the process and preserve it as a tool for future use. Get clear agreed outcomes defined at the start, that is, what will it look like or sound like when we have the outcome. We need to know how we will know we have been successful.

Reward systems based on these guidelines can have immense value and be great motivators for students. Such approaches encourage students to strive for goals and respond appropriately in class. There are other aspects of the learning zone that must also be managed to maintain self-esteem while empowering children to take risks.

## Six key motivators

We all have internal motivators. We pay attention to certain stimuli while we ignore others. In classrooms, if we are to keep students on task, it is vital to trigger their intrinsic motivation in order to channel their energy. In a group of 30 students, the motivators are multiple and will vary across the group. What follows are the six key motivators for students and suggestions as to how to provide for them.

1   Achievement-focused or avoidance-focused

2   Agreement or disagreement centred

3   Self or others

4   Visual, auditory or kinesthetic (VAK)

5   Rational-logical or holistic

6   Immersion or tracking

What do each of these motivators mean in practice?

# 1 Achievement-focused or avoidance-focused

Some children are motivated by moving towards positive achievement – for example, gaining a perfect score on a piece of work – we call them achievement-focused (AC-F). Others are motivated by an avoidance-focus (AV-F). In other words, they move away from a fear of what will happen if they do not try hard; for example, if I do not complete my picture by break, then I will not get any break time. In classrooms, we have children who are strongly AV-F and those who are strongly AC-F; similarly there can also be combined motivations. The important point to remember is that if we use AV-F approaches with children who are strongly AC-F, then they will not work!

How to manage this in the classroom.

- Notice what motivates your most challenging individuals when they are with others. Are they motivated by achieving something or by avoiding something? Change your approach accordingly and remember that these motivations may be context dependent, so consider when a student does a specific activity or behaves in a certain way. What is their motivation then?

- Let go of any beliefs that you have that children do not deserve rewards, or do not deserve sanctions. At the end of the day they have their own motivation strategy and if you want to move them forward, then you will have to match their strategy. It is generally considered that an AC-F strategy is a healthier one in terms of minimizing negative stress.

- Be aware of your own motivation strategy. Are you strongly one or the other, or a little of both? Without awareness of this you may find yourself using your own strategy to motivate someone with a different strategy—and this does not work!

# 2 Agreement or disagreement centred

Some people you meet in life are agreement centred, that is, they tend to agree with what you think. Others are disagreement centred and tend to disagree with what you think. Others combine both. A person who is strongly disagreement centred will use phrases in conversation such 'Ah, yes but what about this…', or 'I don't see it like that … I see it like this'. Agreement-centred learners tend to accept wisdom and ideas more readily than disagreement-centred learners. Disagreement-centred learners need greater levels of justification for why a situation is as it is.

How to manage this in the classroom.

- Provide opportunities for learners to discuss issues and express their opinions.

- Engage learners in deciding what they want to get out of the lesson based around the lesson outcomes you have planned. Disagreement-centred learners will want things other than those you want. By getting them to express those other needs, you hear them and may be able to provide aspects of those needs too.

- Use language patterns that present a disagreement pattern so that in order to disagree with you, the student has to agree with you; for example, 'You probably won't agree with me but I think...'. In this situation, in order for the student to disagree with you, they actually have to accept your point of view.

## 3 Self or others

In this motivation framework, some learners are interested in themselves and some are interested in other people and what they are doing and thinking. A strongly self-motivated person tends to be highly insular and prefers to work alone. In groups, they may withdraw or, alternatively, strive for their own agenda at the cost of the group. Other-motivated learners are intensely interested in what others have to say and learn a great deal from being with others.

How to manage this in the classroom.

- Create variety in your activities so that students have the opportunity over the course of a lesson to work in groups, pairs and alone. This ensures that self- and other-motivated learners have their needs met.

- Create protocols and teach them to children for behaving in groups, including an awareness of what active listening is like, and provide roles for people to perform while part of a group; for example, scribe, time-keeper, umpire, summarizer.

- Model both kinds of behaviour in yourself in the class so that students can see the benefits of being self-reflective (that is, in solving individual problems) and others-motivated (that is, in getting things done in a team).

## 4 Visual, auditory or kinesthetic (VAK)

Varying your classroom delivery in terms of the sensory filters that learners possess is critical. While there is much myth and hearsay related to VAK, the way in which learners perceive their surroundings is mediated by preferences for visual (what they see), auditory (what they hear and say) and kinesthetic (what they do and feel). Consequently, a classroom environment that provides opportunities to experience and demonstrate learning through all three of these sensory channels is a powerful one. Supplying activities that over a course of a lesson provide for VAK ensures that all motivators are stimulated.

How to manage this in your classroom:

- Work at providing entry activities for the moment that a student comes into the classroom, vary the entry activity according to the VAK preferences over time. Do the same in the plenary part of your lesson and make the plenary activity different in terms of VAK preference to your entry activity. Make it clear at the start what activities are on offer in the lesson that day, so students know that they will have their needs met.

- Audit your lessons over time. Check whether there is any bias apparent over a month or a term in the kinds of preferences you are providing for. This can reveal your own preferences and help you plan a more rounded provision for your students.

- Collect ideas from others for activities that meet VAK needs. Look out for classroom activities that can match all three learning preferences in one go. Visit www.visionforlearning.co.uk for free resource ideas for learning activities. *Accelerated Learning: A User's Guide* (Smith et al. 2003) is an invaluable treasure trove of learning activities.

## 5 Rational-logical or holistic

Some students need the details and some like the overview. Those that prefer and, indeed, crave the intricate details of exactly how they will carry out the activity, project or task, are rational-logical motivated learners. On the other hand, those who like to have a more general overview are the holistic learners. This relates vaguely to a somewhat oversimplified theory referred to as left- and right-brain theory. Rational-logical motivated learners tend to be fearful if they do not have every detail and crave a set of steps and have all resources to hand and in one place. Holistic motivated learners prefer to work in groups and to find out for themselves through exploratory activities, research and discussion. These learners are de-motivated by heavy reference to detail.

How to manage this in the classroom.

- Meet both motivational needs at the start of your lesson by giving an overview of what students will learn and, in broad terms, how they will learn it. Then provide the specific details of the outcomes and what will happen and when.

- For holistic-motivated learners, build in humour, connecting activities, such as reviewing previous learning, lots of group-work, ensure there is plenty of variety and, where possible, have them move around to locate resources and information from sources around the room or further afield.

- For rational-logical learners, make task instructions really clear, provide time for learners to organize themselves before commencing a task. Provide exact criteria for the outcomes of tasks, and exemplar work where practical.

- Managing both kinds of motivations in a lesson might seem tricky, but it is essentially about ensuring that within a lesson there is a mixture of both sets of needs. If you are clear at the beginning about what they will be doing, learners can see that there is something in it for them.

## 6 Immersion or tracking

The final motivator classification to explore is to do with experience of time. Some learners are able to get totally absorbed in learning activities and forget about time; these are known as immersion-motivated learners. In this motivation frame, learners enter a state called flow that enables them to be highly creative and very relaxed.

Tracking-motivated learners are constantly aware of time and pressurize themselves to complete tasks within a given timeframe. They may be unrealistic about the time it takes to complete an outcome and tend to be highly driven individuals. There are advantages and disadvantages to both kinds of time-related motivations.

How to manage this in the classroom.

- Above all be aware. Students who are strongly immersion focused will become frustrated if their flow is broken, and this needs sensitive handling at times when bells toll and you really need them to pack away! Tracking-motivated learners sometimes requires support in ensuring that the quality of their product is sufficient, because they create time pressures for themselves that may interfere with the outcomes.

- Over the course of a topic, scheme of work or half term, ensure that there are opportunities for these time-related motivators to be triggered. The challenge in most classrooms is to allow sufficient immersion motivation time, in part because of the pressures of the curriculum and in part because many teachers are tracking focused themselves due to the nature of schools.

These six motivational categories are outlined here to give you some pointers to analyse the needs of your students. Additionally, they exist to help you to plan varied and interesting lessons. If you plan to provide the full variety of motivators over time, you are sure to meet even more of your learners' motivational needs even more of the time.

## What is in it for me?

As a student, if your teacher has provided you with a variety of learning experiences and, on the whole, a reasonable range of your motivators are triggered, you are going to feel energized and excited about your learning experiences. Every child who has ever walked into a lesson has had a question on their mind, deep in their unconscious: 'What is in it for me?' This means that as your students walk into your lessons, they are looking for evidence to conclude that there is much in it for them or else they are going to need to create something of their own to get enjoyment in the lesson. Energy spent early in your relationship with students in meeting their motivators allows you to build the expectation that your lessons are worth engaging with. The other question that children ask themselves unconsciously is: 'Is his/her lesson worth behaving for?' A powerful question when you ask it of yourself: 'Is my lesson worth behaving for?'

Perhaps managing behaviour is not really about managing behaviour at all. Perhaps it is really about managing motivation. I believe it is. When you focus on motivating your learners, their natural exuberance and passion for fun is channelled into the learning. It is this that engages them and draws them into the learning zone.

The six motivator categories discussed earlier provide a framework for planning for difference in learners' motivations. It must also be pointed out that there are some constants when it comes to motivation. The following elements are important to all learners:

- Novelty– that there is newness and an element of the unusual.
- Humour – which is generated through the activity and not at the expense of another.
- Curiosity – that there is awe and a sense of wonder and speculation.
- Challenge – that there is something to aspire to and to achieve.
- Fun – to experience the positive emotions of enjoyment.
- The positive attention of another person – perhaps the most powerful motivator of all.

## Ten ways to ensure your lesson is worth behaving for

1  Always give the big picture *and* the detail of the lesson: what we will be learning and how we will be doing the learning.

2  Plan for variety and to provide for the three key sensory preferences of visual, auditory and kinesthetic learning.

3  Explain the benefits in terms of what students will know and what they will experience in your lesson.

4  At the beginning of the lesson, encourage students to reflect on what success will look like, feel like and sound like at the end of the lesson.

5  Structure learning so that it is chunked down into manageable steps.

6  Give at least four opportunities for students to experience the learning (use Alistair Smith's four-part Accelerated Learning Cycle: www.alite.co.uk).

7  Engage students' curiosity with unusual questions, or the use of behaviours, objects, pictures or sounds that encourage problem solving and challenge. For example, revealing a picture bit by bit through a lesson with the questions, 'What is it?' 'How does it relate to our lesson today?'

8  Set the expectation that your classroom is about learning by providing an activity for students to do as soon as they arrive (for a selection of such activities visit www.visionforlearning.co.uk and follow the learning resources link).

9  Adopt a regular focus and review process throughout the lesson so it is broken down into short bursts of high-level concentration.

10  Leave them on a high at the end of the lesson – how will you ensure that every single student leaves feeling successful?

## Beliefs and the positive attention of another

Providing positive attention is a chief motivator for children. It communicates belief in them and shows that we care. In a number of surveys where students are asked 'What makes a good teacher?', a featured response in the top five answers is 'that they care about me'.

Consider the following situation.

### 'How was your grandma?'

A student called Mary comes into school on a Friday and persistently tries to tell her teacher that her grandmother is visiting her this weekend. She is really looking forward to it. The teacher's time is short, the numeracy lesson is about to begin. She asks the girl to sit down. The weekend comes and goes. On Monday morning when Mary comes into school, her teacher sees her and says: 'Mary how was your grandma?' Mary beams and is delighted. A short exchange between the two further cements a strong mutual respect.

What this short exchange has provided for this young girl is a recognition that her teacher cares enough to ask her about something she is motivated by. At a deep level, this kind of care suggests that her teacher believes in her enough to ask. The beliefs that we hold as teachers about our learners can have profound positive and negative impacts upon students' self-esteem, performance and behaviour.

Now consider this situation.

### A sporting chance

A golfer approaches the next tee and notices a large lake just in front of the target green. He places his current 'best' ball back in his golf bag and takes out three old balls placing the first one on the tee. He focuses on the lake that he wishes to avoid, and he drives off. A few seconds and the ball is in the lake, closely followed, of course, by the next two balls.

Where you focus is where you head. Or another way of referring to this is: 'You get what you expect.' The power of belief and expectation should not be underestimated in the field of learning. It is extremely well documented in sport and other professions. There is good evidence of poor performance directly related to prior expectation. What is in the mind will even change physical responses as it did in our golfer. Your self-talk (what you say to yourself in your head) and your internal visual representations of the world around you shape it.

Now consider a classroom example of the above in action.

### It's not what you say, it's the way that you say it

A teacher is calling the register. She gets to the fourth name down, Peter, and there is no answer from the child. For a moment the teacher feels a sense of relief as she sees Peter as a challenging child and a day without him in class would make life easier for everyone; even the rest of the children visibly relax. A few moments later Peter walks into the room just as the register is finished. The teacher chooses her words carefully, as she prepares to speak to Peter. She turns to Peter and welcomes him, 'Hello Peter, come and sit down'. The sharp tone of voice and body language (dismissive hand and eye movements) reflects the teacher's true disappointment however.

These are the messages that Peter receives whenever he interacts with his teacher. Subtle signs but, nonetheless, picked up by the boy. These messages are already creating this child's negative internal image of himself. What we think about our children, we unconsciously communicate to them. This is helpful when we have empowering thoughts about them, but can be destructive if the reverse is true. As we learned earlier in this book, self-esteem is a key factor in developing positive learning behaviours in schools. When self-esteem is undermined by a teacher's apparent negative beliefs about the child, it can have a devastating effect on that child's outlook with that teacher.

Consider the two approaches in the following situation.

### There's a right way and a wrong way

- Student arrives for detention after school.
- Teacher looks up from marking.
- Teacher: 'Oh it's you. I didn't think you would come.'
- Student is further assured that the teacher does not think much of him.

An alternative could be:
Teacher: 'Hello Peter, thank you for coming to your detention. It's good to know I can rely on you.'

In the alternative approach, the student receives affirmation for doing the right thing in turning up and the teacher rewards with praise a behaviour he expects to continue – that of reliability. He can refer back to this at later points in the year too, to build the boy's self-esteem. The teacher is not only supporting the development of the child's positive self-image, he is also reinforcing his own positive beliefs about the boy. Words that reinforce old patterns of behaviour do not help people to change; catching them doing it right and pointing out the positive behaviour are more likely to bring about change.

When managing children with challenging behaviour, it is crucial to be open to challenging your own beliefs about them. A few unpleasant exchanges between you and a student can soon colour your perceptions and give way to the formation of beliefs about them and attitudes towards them. This is a natural human response but in the professional situation we need to be aware of this and be prepared to challenge unhelpful beliefs.

## Beliefs and attitudes

Beliefs are ideas we no longer question. They are the software upon which our minds operate. They form throughout our lives from our earliest to our last moments. They are plastic and can be reprogrammed when we change how we see a situation, when we change what we say to ourselves about it and when we change what we feel. Beliefs are, on the whole, generalizations, that is, they are rules that we form to make our lives easier. Your conscious short-term memory finds it difficult to hold more than seven plus or minus two pieces of information and so makes sense of complex information by simplifying it. The result is a belief. Something we take to be true. In reality, it is not the reality, just a perception of the actual circumstances.

Some common examples of beliefs in school are:

- I'm a good teacher.
- That child is a delight to work with.
- He is hateful and there is nothing redeemable in him.
- They are bottom band kids ... what can you expect?
- He's from the estate (unsaid: 'There is therefore no point trying with him, it's a lost cause.').

Sometimes in jest and sometimes to excuse poor performance, these comments nibble away at expectations and these beliefs become a shared excuse for lowered expectation. Thinking such as this tends to ensure that poor expectations will be lived up to or down to. In consequence, difficult though it is, we do need to probe and gently challenge these excuses in ourselves and others. In ourselves, this is an awareness shift. Paying more attention to our spoken comments, humour and internal thought processes helps us to identify and eliminate disempowering beliefs. One great point about beliefs is that once you consciously pay attention to them and start to question them, they are quite fragile. This makes changing them relatively easy. We must remember, however, that our reptilian brain can sometimes kick in if challenging a belief means pressing the 'hot buttons' we referred to in the previous chapter. In some people, the challenging of disempowering beliefs can be done most effectively using gently challenging questions, such as:

- What do you mean specifically by that?
- How do you know that that is true?
- What causes you to choose to believe that this is true?

The framework of a belief begins to weaken when it is questioned. Some beliefs may need more questioning than others. Suffice to say, you need to pick your moment and have a good relationship to really challenge someone's beliefs.

Our role in education is to maximize the time students spend being successful in the learning zone. It is necessary to provide challenge and support for students and this is done through a number of key approaches:

- Ensuring that there is a well-established safe zone.
- Personalizing rewards linked to genuine positive attention from those whom they respect.
- Building and maintaining self-esteem.
- Having high positive expectations.
- Holding and communicating a strong belief in a student's ability to improve.
- Holding a willingness to challenge our own disempowering beliefs towards students.
- Providing highly motivating learning experiences.

In the next chapter, we move on further with the Learning Zone Model to explore the anxiety zone, discovering how to avoid it and what to do if students venture into it.

## Summary

- There are six key factors in engaging and motivating learners.

- There are six key motivators for learners. Awareness of these, and planning lessons to provide a variety of experiences, keeps learners engaged and encourages learning behaviours.

- Self-belief is critical to learners being able to operate in the learning state. If we wish to promote positive learning behaviours and minimize unwanted behaviours, we need to promote self-esteem in our learners so they have a secure, safe state as a foundation for risk-taking.

- We get more of what we focus on. Therefore we should be spending time focusing on developing learning behaviours rather than managing poor behaviour.

- Our expectations shape our outcomes. Rethinking our expectations helps us to use empowering communication in words, tone of voice and body language.

## Self-coaching insight questions

- What do you genuinely believe about your most challenging students?

- What are you communicating to them?

- Ask someone else to watch you interacting with students and to jot down notes for you on body language, tone of voice and language. Ask for them to report only what they see or hear, and avoid internal judgement on this. Then respond to these questions:

  → What patterns are you noticing?

  → What underlying beliefs or excuses are you aware of in some cases?

  → What is empowering about the feedback you have?

  → How can you use this feedback to develop relationships further?

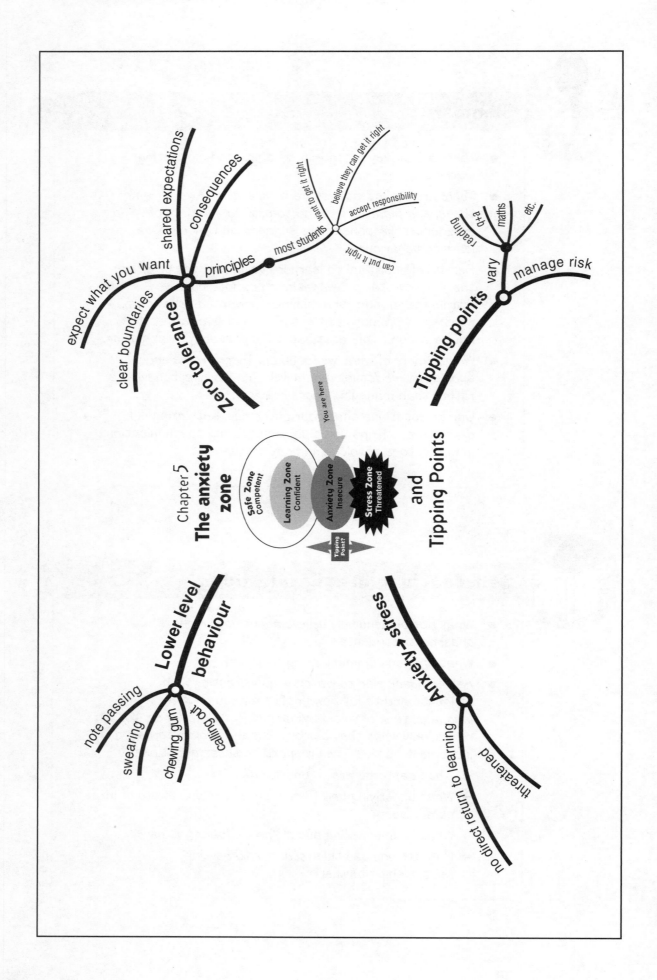

**Chapter 5**

# The anxiety zone and tipping points

" *If you don't know where you are going, any road will take you there.* "

## In this chapter you will:

- learn about the nature of the anxiety zone.

- understand tipping points and how being aware of them helps learners avoid moving into the stress zone.

- understand approaches to maintaining a supportive learning climate.

- discover a simple model for managing tipping points in students.

## Preview questions

- In an average school week, what can happen to send you into high states of anxiety?

- How do you respond to others in that anxiety state?

- What kind of self-talk goes on in your head when you are in that state?

- What are you doing that you do not normally do?

- What are you not doing that you normally do?

- What patterns do you notice and how do they connect with learner behaviours in classrooms?

## The anxiety zone

Imagine you are in the middle of a stimulating and exciting lesson with all the motivators triggered, yet you still get unacceptable behaviour from students that is threatening the learning process. Your expectations are not being met, despite all your routines and rituals. Some students of the time will get it wrong. So what happens then?

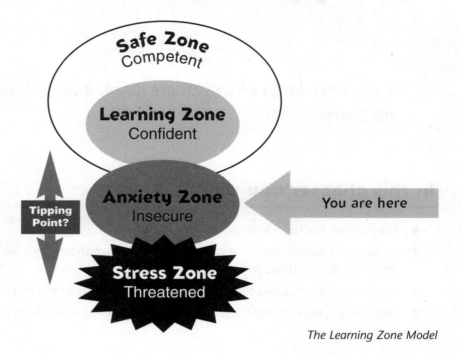

*The Learning Zone Model*

The reason why children lapse is either that they are bored and under-engaged because they are too much in the safe zone, or they are uncertain and unsupported and move into the anxiety zone. The anxiety zone presents itself as a series of lower level behaviours that compromise learning. They include:

- talking while the teacher is talking to the class
- passing notes between themselves
- answering the teacher back
- swearing
- chewing gum
- calling out inappropriately
- rudeness towards teacher or other students
- lower level physical bullying
- name calling
- non-compliance with requests
- surliness.

These behaviours represent the majority of lapses from expectations in classrooms. The stress zone that lies beyond the anxiety zone is where the really extreme behaviour exists. The stress zone is the place where students are uncontrollably violent, physically and verbally, and where they are themselves out of control. We will explore how to deal with these extreme situations in Chapter 6.

Challenging Behaviour – A fresh look at promoting positive learning behaviours

What follows in this chapter is an exploration of the principles for managing children when they enter the anxiety zone. The specific strategies that can be used to resolve situations are given in Chapter 6. Before the strategies are used, it is essential that the operating principles are correct.

# Zero tolerance to maintain

In my experience, expecting what you want is about 80 per cent of actually getting it. This leads to the operation of an effective 'zero tolerance' policy. Zero tolerance simply means that you go all out for your expectations.

The first rule for achieving zero tolerance is to be absolutely clear about what is acceptable and keep to it. You will have already established these expectations through the earlier work in this book. At the risk of over-emphasis, I encourage colleagues to spend a good deal of time adjusting and clarifying their expectations. It really is time well spent, as once the point of clarification is established, it becomes clear what the vision is for the child, group or school. A shared set of expectations leaves no grey areas and it is obvious to everyone what is required, what it looks like and how students will behave.

Naturally, if you have certain expectations, there needs to be consequences for any lapses. The language is all-important here: consequences, not sanctions nor punishments. Punitive approaches hold certain difficulties. They have a tendency to remove the responsibility for the behaviour from the individual and place it with the teacher or teaching assistant. This allows offenders to put the blame outside themselves. Students who understand the expectation lapse–consequence connection take more responsibility for their actions.

Schools that use control based on punishment tend to create a 'them and us' mindset in students. Where punishment-driven management exists, students are often behaving well through fear. The difficulty with this is that fear can actually provoke inappropriate behaviours. If fear tips them into reptilian brain processing, children respond with the fight, flight, flock and freeze responses outlined in Chapter 2. This can place students in such schools on the edge of the stress zone and most certainly in the anxiety zone.

So what is effective in achieving zero tolerance of non-learning behaviours? Some basic principles apply in seeking zero tolerance; such as  for example, the vast majority of students:

- want to get it right.
- believe that they can get it right.
- accept that they are responsible for their own behaviour.
- even if they do get it wrong, believe they can put it right.

The first stage of wanting to get it right is about establishing ownership of what right is and this takes us back to our and their expectations for successful learning.

# From anxiety zone to stress zone: tipping points

Learning, by definition, is risky. It involves having new experiences and approaching situations in different ways. We may not know what will happen. There are unknowns and there are risks. Sometimes those risks may involve physical harm, and sometimes a risk of failure, success or humiliation. These risks can allow us to take on new models of thinking, new skills and fresh knowledge. They can also lead us to experiencing anxiety. Anxiety occurs when the learning experiences are too challenging. The result of failure by the teacher to manage the challenge can lead from anxiety to full-blown stress. Hence, the student moves from the learning zone to the anxiety zone and then to the stress zone. We are now going to explore the interface between the anxiety zone and the stress zone. We call this interface the tipping point.

To illustrate the concept of the tipping point, consider the following situation as if you were doing it.

### Tipping for a safe ride home: the train journey
Imagine you have to go on a journey late at night on your own on a train and then complete the journey on foot.

As you read the story, notice the point at which you feel nervous, the point you feel unable to complete the journey, the point you become so stressed that you want to be out of the situation altogether and fast, and the point when you would call a taxi.

- You are standing on your own late at night on the platform waiting for the train.
- The train arrives and you step on taking a seat on your own; you notice three other passengers.
- At the next station all the passengers get off and you are left entirely on your own.
- The next station is yours so you step off the train, leave the station and start the walk towards your destination. It is very dark and you appear to be quite alone.
- As you walk, you hear footsteps behind you so you walk quicker.
- The footsteps appear to be catching you up.
- You cross the road and sure enough the footsteps follow you.
- You glance over your shoulder and you notice it is a man.
- You are almost running now and eventually he catches up with you and taps you on your shoulder.

So at what point did you say to yourself 'I'm really scared and I really want to be somewhere else; in other words where was your tipping point? When did you tip into stress zone?

Share this story with a few other people and you will find that we are all different, some people just would not travel on their own late at night at all, others would be fine on the train but not walking and so on. Different people have different tipping points.

Consider these questions in relation to your experience:

- Who is right or wrong?
- Are the people who find the whole idea of going out at night too much and do not begin the journey being over-cautious?
- What makes the difference?
- Why would some people cope better than others?

Would the journey be easier if:

- you had someone with you?
- it was during the day?
- you had been on the journey before?
- you had some way of calling for help, such as a mobile phone or a panic alarm?
- you had something to defend yourself with?
- you felt more able to deal with possible threats?
- you knew more about the journey and the destination?
- you could choose a different mode of transport?
- the reason for the journey was explicit and important; for example, you were trying to see a dying friend and it was the only way to get to them?

## Tipping zones in the classroom

The train journey is a form of risk-taking and each of us has varying tolerance points often based on what we *feel* might happen to us. Our personal tipping point is just as valid as anyone else's, even though they are different. Your tipping point is based on your belief system, not necessarily the actual reality. What you fear dictates your model of acceptable and unacceptable risk.

For many of our learners, the classroom is fraught with unacceptable risks. For some children their tipping points might be:

- the thought of school, even before they get out of bed in the morning.
- walking to school, thinking of the lessons they have that day.
- walking into the playground/building where they are teased/bullied.
- answering a question in front of others.
- a certain teacher's attitude.
- a male teacher, or a female teacher.
- being asked to read.
- being asked to write.
- anything to do with numeracy.

It is important for us as teachers to look back at the behaviour we see in our students and to look for the tipping points. If we can identify them, we can manage them better. It is easy for us to forget how it feels to take the risk of learning as we tend to be far more comfortable with learning than our students. Tasks and experiences that we take for granted as easy may invoke high levels of anxiety for our learners.

How do we make it safer to learn yet still be challenging?

Come back to the train journey and consider the options that could have made the journey easier and apply it to the classroom.

### You had someone with you
Learning is so much safer when you can share the experience and work with others, yet we still insist that learners learn alone for between 80 and 90 per cent of our teaching. Plan for paired work.

### It was during the day
We all prefer to be able to see where we are going, yet too often the only person who knows where the lesson is going and the key points along the way is the teacher. Share objectives and the 'route' with the learners both at the beginning and throughout to help them see the destination.

### You had been on the journey before
Scaffold the learning to reassure learners that the journey is not unknown – it links to previous learning and use a consistent structure on which to hang the new content. For example, use a learning cycle that you share with your students.

### You had some way of calling for help, such as a mobile phone or a panic alarm
Teach learners strategies for what to do when they don't know what to do! Scaffold learning in understandable chunks.

### You had something to defend yourself with
Learners need supportive skills to tackle new learning and positive previous learning to move forward. Teach them to reflect back on their successes and draw on their strengths to help them in new situations. Model this behaviour yourself.

### You felt more able to deal with possible threats
Successful learners have high self-esteem that builds resilience to failure. Create regular opportunities at the beginning and endings of lessons, topics, terms and days for pupils to review their successes and reflect on strategies for coping when they get stuck.

### You knew more about the journey and the destination
Structure the learning process with clear explicit guidelines about what and how we are learning today. Be really clear about the processes that you will employ and the activities students will do.

### You could choose a different mode of transport
The destination may be the same but build in choice about how to get there. Encourage different ways to learn and ways to demonstrate your learning. For example, enable students to have a visual, auditory or kinesthetic activity to choose from to review their learning

**The reason for the journey was explicit and important; for example, you were trying to see a dying friend and it was the only way to get to them?**
Make sure you sell the benefits of the learning both the 'what' and the 'how'!

Much of the process of managing children away from the anxiety zone is about managing risk. A combination of the approaches above will reduce the anxiety levels of children and enable challenge but not at the expense of safety. One common source of anxiety for students is a well-used classroom strategy of teachers posing questions to the whole class for public response. We will use this as an example to take the anxiety zone and tipping point concept into the classroom situation.

## Is question time contributing to learning or causing anxiety?

One common tipping point for many pupils is teacher-to-class question and answer. On the surface, it is a quick and easy method for a teacher to assess the knowledge of a group. Look a little deeper, however, and it can be promoting unease, involve very few pupils, feed insecurities and be intensely isolating.

The following is an example (albeit a little exaggerated and crude) by way of illustration.

> The class are listening to their teacher. The teacher asks some questions about what the class have been learning. This could take the form of quite closed questions, such as 'Do you think...?', 'Can you name...?'. There's almost a teacher–pupil telepathic capability assumed by the teacher.

**Teacher**  Who can tell me something about the character in the story called Fred?

> Maybe 30 per cent of pupils put their hands up. Some pupils are told by the teacher to put their hands down as she wants some answers from those who do not always answer. One pupil with his arm forced high and itching to answer is approached by the teacher.

**Teacher**  Come on John what can you tell me?

**John**  Oh, I forgot!

> Classmates laugh, teacher moves on.

**Teacher**  Mary, your answer please?

> Mary is caught like a rabbit in a headlamp and in her anxiety, says something that is not relevant. The class laugh again. Teacher scolds the class for being unkind.

> Teacher turns to Sally. Sally gives a partial answer.

| Teacher | Almost right Sally! |
|---|---|
| | Finally, the teacher turns to Bill who is looking out the window. |
| Teacher | Bill, your answer? |
| | Bill does not have an answer and for the next few minutes the teacher tells the whole class how badly behaved Bill is. |
| | If Bill has any sense of self, he will see the need to react aggressively to being admonished in front of his classmates. |

For consideration:

- How much learning has taken place here?
- How many of these learners feel supported by the learning process in teacher question time?
- How many pupils have learned how *not* to take part in this learning activity?

It may well be that a high proportion have learned little more from teacher question time than how not to take part. Particularly at post-primary levels, many students will move into anxiety zone and, potentially, stress zone in these situations. This can be made worse by the teacher having her own anxiety zone triggered because very few students are joining in. The teacher might then respond in frustrated and perhaps aggressive ways, thus tipping a few more students away into anxiety and stress.

## Alternative approaches to question time

Let us examine what could support learning rather than tipping pupils into their anxiety zone.

First, consider the purpose of the activity: what is it the teacher wants at teacher question time? What are the expectations and behaviours that represent those expectations?

Perhaps the teacher wants pupils to answer questions so that knowledge and understanding can be assessed. Alongside this, pupils could review their learning and benefit from hearing others' contributions as well as their own.

In teacher question and answer sessions, meaningful learning most often comes from question types that cause pupils to think widely and deeply. Using open-style questions – which generally begin with what, when, where, who, how or why prefixes – stimulates this kind of thinking.

When pupils are asked more open styles of questioning there are a number of steps they potentially could need to take in order to respond:

1 Consider: What does the question mean?

2 Consider: What might be the possible answers?

3 Consider: What words could I use to give my answer?

4   Rehearse that answer and check if it sounds right.

5   Put up my hand to offer an answer.

6   Wait, keeping the answer in my head, until the teacher invites me to respond.

It is probable that this will take many seconds. Pupils are likely to feel uncomfortable risking an answer in front of their contemporaries that is hurriedly formed. The reward for all this work and risk is available to only one in the group, who is chosen by the teacher. The only opportunity to get a second chance is if someone else fails.

How can question and answer sessions be made less risky and become richer learning opportunities for all?

Pupils need support to give an answer to get it right and need structures that help make it happen. A simple adaptation to the above approach can pay dividends:

1   Teacher poses a question and/or writes it on the board.

2   In pairs, pupils are given two minutes to come up with some possible answers to the question. Using the words 'some' and 'possible' reduces stress. They reduce the fear of coming up with a wrong answer while still encouraging challenging thinking.

3   On a given signal, contributions are invited.

As contributions are made, emphasis is then on adding to the possible answer, building on others' contributions thereby teaching pupils more about scaffolding learning.

The likely outcomes are:

●   more contributions

●   more learning

●   greater confidence

●   high challenge, with less risk

●   fewer anxiety and stress zone behaviours in students and teacher.

# Anxiety zone to stress zone: the point of no return

If pupils do reach their tipping point, there can be a tendency for teachers to have their anxiety zones triggered. If teachers unconsciously allow themselves to reach their own tipping point, a situation very quickly escalates. It is possible that a teacher will use voice tone, and verbal and body language to exert and demonstrate 'control' rather than a wish to manage learning. When this happens, any aggression in the teacher will trigger more pupils to become anxious and, in turn, they can reach their tipping points. Before long both teacher and pupils are in the stress zone. From here it is very difficult to return to the learning zone. In addition to careful planning for the learning zone, it is critical for teachers to stay away from their own tipping points. Anxious learners and anxious teachers quickly tip into desperate people operating on their reptilian instincts.

In this chapter we have explored the important concept of the tipping point that occurs when pupils are in a state of anxiety. In the next chapter, we explore a simple approach to managing learners in the anxiety zone.

## Summary

- Everyone has different tipping points that take them further away from learning towards high-level stress.
- Managing the tipping points is partly about observing individuals, but also about proactively considering how we structure high-risk activities in class.
- It is important to realize that activities, experiences and language that we take for granted as acceptable, may be intensely anxiety-invoking for some learners.
- Pairing and sharing work prior to question and answer sessions is one example of managing a high-risk process.

## Self-coaching insight questions

- What kind of activities cause your students to feel most uncomfortable and why? How could you refine your knowledge of this?
- From their responses, how might you scaffold the risk for the most risky activities?
- With your students' help, how could you develop ideas to make risk feel safer?

*In a heated argument we are apt to lose sight of the truth.*

(Publilius Syrus)

# Section 3

# How do we build and maintain learning behaviours?

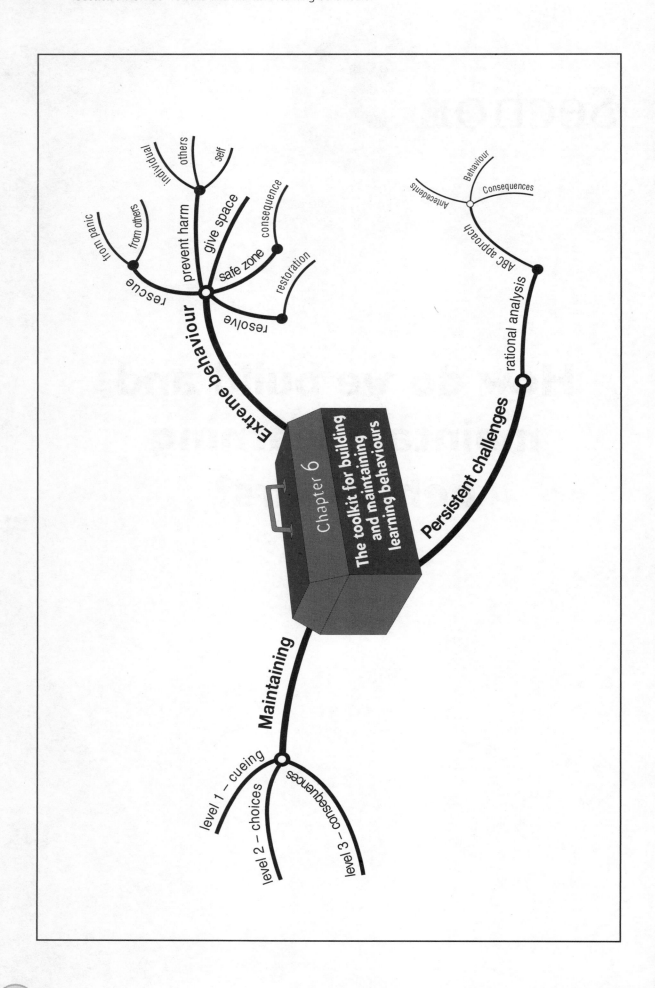

# Chapter 6

# The toolkit for building and maintaining learning behaviours

> *If you have only a hammer in your toolkit, then you have to treat every job like it's a nail.*

## In this chapter you will:

- increase your flexibility in setting high expectations and encouraging learning behaviours.
- access a bank of tools to manage learning more effectively at three levels of intervention.
- be able to select the right tool for the right situation.

## Preview questions

What's in your current toolkit for:
- preventing poor behaviour?
- encouraging positive behaviour?
- managing conflict?
- bringing students back from their tipping points?

## Strategies and the three levels of intervention

In this chapter, you are introduced to a bank of practical strategies you can employ to support learning behaviours and move learners from undesirable states and behaviours back to the learning zone. The earlier chapters contain a description of the Learning Zone Model and emphasize the need to provide a reliable, secure safe zone that allows students to successfully move into the risky area of the learning zone. As previously described, when students move into the learning zone in classrooms, they are exposed to risk. This can cause them to move into the anxiety zone and, in turn, tip into stress. With the right support, using appropriate strategies, we can guide students from anxiety back to learning.

To help you to choose the right strategy for the right situation, the approaches are organized into three levels.

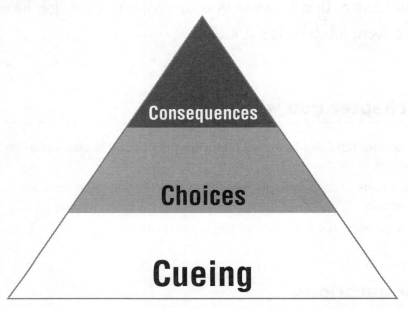

*The Triangle Intervention Model*

**Level 1:** *Cueing – securing and maintaining the learning zone.* Minimal interventions and support that reminds learners of learning expectations.

**Level 2:** *Choices – preventing learning-avoidance and confrontation.* These provide learners with choices about doing the right thing.

**Level 3:** *Consequences.* These are clear consequences that allow students to self-rescue.

What follows are sets of tools, approaches and strategies for use at each of the three levels of intervention.

# Level 1: Cueing – securing and maintaining the learning zone

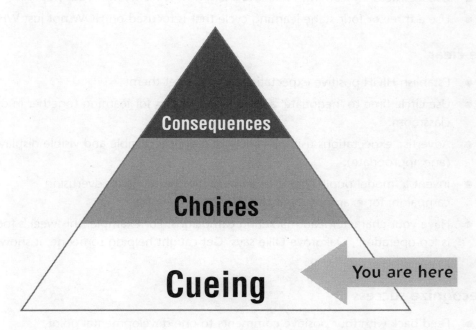

*The Triangle Intervention Model*

Level 1 adult support/intervention is called 'Cueing'. In other words, it covers those things we say and do that prompt a feeling of safety and security in our learners: clear, concise yet flexible boundaries; rules, routines and structures for learning that can be relied on when anxiety looms.

## Strategies
### Be organized

- Ensure resources are readily accessible – always have spare copies and spare equipment, and what about alternatives when equipment is prone to failure?
- Label and count equipment, organize systems to ensure loss is minimal.
- Make a huge fuss about 'accidental' damage and how disappointed you are.
- Set up a system of 'Loan of Equipment' at extortionate interest rates!

### Be prepared

- Plan not just WHAT will be learned but especially HOW it will happen. That means including a plan to manage pupil movement, accessing resources, groupings and so on.
- Have a column in your planning for HOT SPOT Action, that is, note where movement could be a problem and think through a routine to assist a smooth transition. Send pupils to new stations in controlled groupings rather than all at once.

### Ensure a variety of teaching learning styles

- Use VAK notation on your planning.
- Use a structured learning cycle and share how it works with your pupils.
- Use a three or four stage learning cycle that is focused on HOW not just WHAT.

### Be clear

- Establish HIGH positive expectations and market them!
- Use circle time to 'negotiate' a list of expectations for learning together in our classroom.
- Advertise expectations using a variety of highly accessible and visible displays (age appropriate).
- Invent a 'model pupil' character and use him/her in your advertising campaign; for example, Kynaston Kid, Oakgrove Ollie.
- Have your character lead marketing campaigns. For example, this week's focus is 'co-operation', Oakgrove Ollie says 'Get caught helping someone, it shows you care!'

### Recognize success

- Feed back with four positive comments to one developmental point.
- Catch them being good.
- Respond to getting it wrong by focusing on those pupils getting it right – 'Well done this group for settling so quickly.'
- Today I'm looking out for the 'biggest smile'.

### Celebrate success

- Show you value the 'right behaviours' with a wink, a thumbs up.
- Use 'tokens' of appreciation stickers, reward schemes, prizes and so on. Make them 'valued' by being consistent and accessible to all. It is the consistent yet flexible recognition of progress that matters not the value of the 'reward'.

### Express your disappointment but not your negative judgements!

- 'I'm surprised at you for doing *that*, it's just not what I would have expected of you.'
- 'I'm disappointed *that* it has taken so long to clear up. I thought you all had made such progress.'

### Be determined

- Never lower your expectations – look for smaller steps.
- 'Well done, that was better. Now we need to add some accuracy.'
- 'We agreed this was quiet working time. The noise is too much. Let's stick to our agreement.'

- 'We have agreed clear expectations about ... and I'm determined to reach them!'
- 'That behaviour is just not acceptable. What one thing could you do right now to start putting it right?'
- Use 'we' messages:
  - → 'We need quiet so we can work.'
  - → 'We need to move carefully so no one gets hurt.'
  - → 'We need to support each other's learning so we all learn more.'

## Be unusual

- Too much structure and organization becomes mundane – plan to be spontaneous!
- Introduce puppets, dressing up or role play at regular intervals that appear spontaneous!
- Go with the flow – if it suddenly snows, use it – and occasionally abandon the original plan!
- Abandon a day's timetable to focus on a theme. This needs careful planning but they don't know that!

## Be personal

- Add humour (not sarcasm):
  - → Use cartoons and funny stories to illustrate learning.
  - → Have a quote or joke of the day.
  - → Laugh at your mistakes.

- Share appropriate personal interests:
  - → Hobbies that may well relate to their lives, such as fishing, sport and so on.
  - → Minor family details – names, ages of children and tales of what they get up to.
  - → Holiday places where you have been, especially local places that they will know about.
  - → TV programmes you watch.

- Allow your pupils to see you are a learner too:
  - → Talk about 'new' things you are learning about and how you do that.
  - → Discuss books you have read.
  - → Mention things you do to prepare their lessons.

- Make mistakes and laugh about them:
  - → Play spot my error.
  - → Plan mistakes so they can catch you out.

## Prepare your pupils

Supply carefully organized routines to deal with the obvious and the not so obvious – getting pupils in, getting them settled, getting them working in groups and independently.

- Routines that deal with their belongings.
- Early bird starters, that is, something to do as you enter the classroom – mini challenges and so on – that may have a connection or not with the day's learning.
- Map your positioning in the classroom to ritualize the behaviour you want; for example, when you want them to stop and listen, consider where you stand to achieve this.
- Use some ritualistic stop signals and then change them occasionally to add more interest.
- Make some routines FUN, especially at the beginning, to sell them. Do not forget to freshen them up every now and again. For example, in the ICT suite get them to stop, leave the equipment alone and listen by saying 'Put one hand in the air, put the other hand in the air, bring them together and give yourself a clap. Now arms folded and listen.'

Teach them what to do when they do not know what to do!

- Teach and display a strategy appropriate to pupils of knowing what to do when you are 'stuck'; for example, ask a neighbour, ask a teaching assistant, use a reference point, go to the help point in the room manned by TA or trustee student. Different subjects will need to develop 'What to do when you don't know what to do' that are age and curriculum appropriate.

Ignore nothing–*choose* a response and show your disapproval by:

- giving a disapproving look.
- shaking your head.
- giving a thumbs down.
- moving in the student's direction, standing closer but saying nothing.
- raising your eyebrows.
- stopping, looking, arms folded, pausing and moving on saying 'Thank you' as the unacceptable behaviour ceases.
- saying 'Excuse me', pausing then continuing. The pause needs silence and brevity. Avoid saying 'I'm waiting', that is stating the obvious and gives control of the pause to the student/s!

Keep moving and scanning.

- If you are physically static for too long, students can easily avoid getting caught!
- Use your eyes so you can nip things in the bud with the 'teacher look'!

Analyse your view of the learning environment and that of all the pupils.

● What you think they can see and hear may not be reality! Sit where they sit and check out how clear their view is.

● Can they hear you? Volume and monotony matter!

Use careful seating plans and groupings that assist you in being vigilant.

● Pay attention to aptitudes needed in a grouping not just academic ability.

● Be aware of social pecking orders and their corrosive effect on learning groups.

● Every time the class re-group, they have to re-establish their social position – too much change depletes time on learning.

● Teach pupils how to share their learning.

● Teach skills and aptitudes for group working.

● Is your seating plan only about control? Where is your plan for learning?

Protect your buttons.

● Know what presses your buttons and rehearse your responses.

● Create your own phrases and actions that you feel comfortable with and practise them!

● What is your hot spot? What do you say or do to deflect attacks?

Be who you want them to be!

● Model the expectations you have of them.

● Politeness? If you are interrupted by another teacher or pupil while working with a pupil, apologize to the pupil for talking to someone else when it was their time. Use a non-verbal signal to indicate you are going to return to them.

● Open doors for pupils and expect them to say thank you.

● Acknowledge pupils' good manners by saying thank you.

● Never talk over a pupil, especially when it is negative behaviour that is being discussed.

● Stop other adults from showing rudeness to your pupils.

When you fall below standard, apologize.

● 'Sorry I had to walk away when you were talking to me, I needed to deal with … You have my attention now.'

● If you end up having to shout, make statements afterwards, such as 'I would much rather talk to you sensibly than have to shout to get your attention.'

● When you get it 'wrong', be prepared to put it right.

● 'Sorry I haven't managed to mark your books, I'll make sure it's done in time for next lesson.'

● 'It wasn't fair of me to say you are all in detention, so I am going to rethink who needs to attend.'

● Try to avoid justifying your mistakes – that is what they do and you do not like it!

# Level 2: Choices – preventing learning-avoidance and confrontation

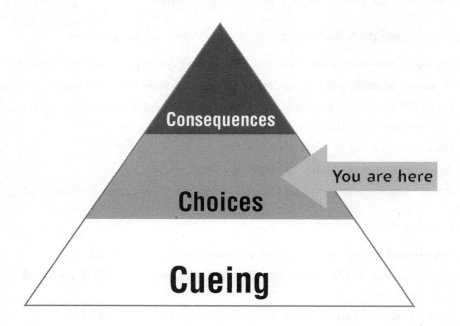

*The Triangle Intervention Model*

At this level, we are dealing with pupils in their anxiety zone. Here pupils begin to feel insecure and lack the confidence to accept the risk-taking of the learning zone. Level 2 interventions lead students back to the learning zone, avoiding their slide into the stress zone and minimizing confrontation.

By its very nature, this anxiety zone requires greater assertiveness on behalf of the lead learner to redirect potentially confrontational behaviours from occurring while also providing vulnerable pupils with a sense of security at a time when they are already feeling vulnerable. Therefore, the emphasis should be on the provision of clearly stated choices rather than ultimatums.

Level 2 interventions or responses must lie firmly on a bed of Level 1 cueing techniques if they are to be effective, as they are designed to return pupils to learning. Level 2 responses are teacher actions and interventions. There are some important principles that underlie the use of the techniques that follow.

## Level 2 principles

When pupils are in their anxiety zone and close to their tipping point, they are in danger of moving into their stress zone. Your task is to prevent them going there. In a few cases, the pupil may well want to take you there too. Some pupils may also want to take other pupils with them. Responding to all of this requires a cool clear head on the teacher's part.

There are five main principles of level 2 intervention techniques:

● Prevent pupils getting so close to the tipping point that they will experience an overwhelming sense of anxiety.

● Restore pupils' own faith in their ability to avoid the high anxiety rather than taking total control of them.

● Stop pupils making the wrong choices and care enough to say no.

● Provide an either/or option.

● Avoid punitive consequences.

In recognizing this balance between inadvertently pushing pupils into the stress zone and making too many decisions for them, we need to give them space to think and decide what to do. Whatever the technique here at the tipping point, we must create the space for both pupil and teacher to make the right decision. It is crucial that we physically and psychologically create that space simply by using a walk away or pause. This is not the time to decide for them but rather to enable them to think for themselves. When you give them choices, give them time to think about the options.

Strategies at level 2 fall into two categories:

● Pre-challenge rescue techniques.

● Responses to behaviour that challenges our learning environment.

## Pre-challenge rescue techniques

These are required because you notice that a pupil or group of pupils are becoming restless – you act before they tip into anxiety.

● 'Pens down everyone we need a fidget moment.'

● 'Hang on, let's stop for a moment. I need to explain this task more clearly.'

● 'Mary, just stop for a moment. I need you to take a message next door.' (The note says to the teacher next door 'Mary just needs five mins to calm down. Thanks!')

## Responses to behaviour that challenges our learning environment

● 'The noise in this room is above our agreed limit. Either you lower your voices or we will have to work without talking. Show me you can get this right.'

● 'I'm disappointed with this group. You can either settle now and complete this work before break or stay in at break to finish it. I'll keep an eye out to see which choice you make!' (Then walk away.)

● 'John, it is not OK to push people. You need to put that right. Take two or three minutes to decide what you need to do about it. I will come back for your decision in three minutes.'

● 'When you have finished clearing up, then you can go to break.'

● 'I know other people haven't finished but right now I'm concerned about you.'

● 'Mary, look at this "consequence note". At the moment it says you will have to stay in at break to finish your work but you now have five minutes to choose to finish your work or take the consequence. It's up to you.' If Mary does finish the work, she gets to tear up the consequence note and bin it!

## Level 3: Consequences

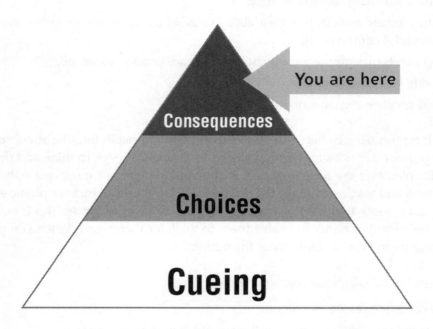

*The Triangle Intervention Model*

Level 3 consequences are required if, despite creating positive climates for learning and establishing flexible redirection at level 2, pupils still make the wrong choices. Sometimes they feel so challenged that they tip into the stress zone and require firm and assertive support.

Although we endeavour to avoid reaching this stress zone, where no learning can take place, this is not always within our control. It is our role to rescue pupils who reach this point where they are out of control. We need to support them to return them to the safe zone. Only from there can we bring them back into learning again.

The challenge for teachers here is to be assertive without aggression. We also need to ensure that the pupils take ownership of their behaviour and therefore the consequences of it in due course.

Initially, we will look at responses that are sequential, that is, what to do when pupils do not respond appropriately to the options offered by interventions at level 2 (Choices). It is important to remember here that level 3 interventions form the smallest part of our day-to-day repertoire of responses. If we drift into regimes that rely heavily on consequences, we probably need to examine how established our safe zone is and how well we are operating our learning zone.

## Making level 3 interventions work

When using level 3 responses, you need to be aware that the pupils needs:

- to be guided back to a safe zone in order to return to learning.
- to learn that confrontational responses do not achieve success.
- support so that they are capable of making the right choices.
- to understand that making the wrong choices is their responsibility and that consistent consequences will follow.
- to be given the opportunity to provide restoration to who or what they have hurt, damaged or interrupted.

It is tempting at level 2 to add the threat of consequences. It is important to be careful that at level 2 any mention of consequences is non-threatening and that there is a way the pupils can avoid this by making the right choices.

For example, you may be tempted to say at level 2 choices: 'If you don't finish your work now, you will be kept in at break and made to do it then!' It may be the teacher's intention to communicate that the student could choose to work now or stay in at break, but often all that is heard by the student are the words: '...kept in at break and made to do it then!'

It might come as no surprise that some students on hearing a threat will defend their corner with a confrontational response of: 'You can't make me...'. This will tempt your brain to respond with: 'Oh yes I can.' Which, of course, you cannot.

## Principles of effective level 3 consequences

### Level 3 can be a starting point

Although the three levels can be sequential, there are times when level 3 needs to be the starting point. Faced with extreme behaviour, that is, those pupils that arrive in the stress zone, consequences may need to happen immediately. They should always, however, lead back to the safe zone and then to cueing or choices once more.

### They are seen as fair

They confirm a natural sense of justice and are transparent, yet focused on the individual circumstances and context of the misdemeanour.

### They are consistent yet reflect fairness

No favouritism is shown, yet they are responsive to the circumstances.

### They are enforceable

Empty threats are pointless and undermine our credibility.

### They are relevant

The 'punishment fits the crime' and focuses on the right choice next time.

### They promote a sense of personal responsibility for our actions

'I made the wrong choice and I can do something about it now and in the future', rather than encouraging a blame culture. A restoration element exists – 'you broke it, you fix it'.

## They encourage a sense of positive self-worth

'I made a mistake, but I can put it right', rather than 'I must make sure I don't get caught next time'.

Finally, the most effective consequences act as a deterrent, and rely on the fact that pupils believe they are very likely to get caught. If pupils are always getting away with misdemeanours, the consequences lose their effectiveness. This reinforces the need for vigilance at level 1 to cue desirable behaviour.

# Level 3 strategies

Level 3 strategies come into play when students have reached their tipping point and crossed over into the stress zone. The following strategies include behavioural approaches and positive language patterns. You need to choose those that are most appropriate in your circumstances. What follows are just suggestions. Using the principles outlined above, you will be able to adapt the ideas and also bring in ideas of your own. You need to decide what is possible in your circumstances and invent for yourself consequences that are relevant to your circumstances. The major difference at level 3 from the other levels is that the teacher makes statements rather than offering choices.

For the purposes of manageability, we will divide the consequences into five areas. These areas cover both classroom and wider school interventions at level 3:

- in classrooms
- loss of privileges
- thinking time
- internal exclusion
- external exclusion.

### In classrooms

'John you are not making the right choice. Go and work on your own in the quiet corner for five minutes.'

- Use a timer to stick to the plan. This may need to be a pupil-friendly visual timer so the child is clear how long five minutes is. Younger pupils may need shorter time targets, such as two minutes.

- Be prepared for any attempts the pupil makes to argue with this. Assertively restate your request and repeat, avoiding any debate.

- At this point there are no choices – we have passed level 2 intervention now.

- Make statements using the 'broken record' technique and keep language brief: 'This desk for five minutes'. Still allow some space for thinking but keep this brief and only interrupted by your 'broken record' statement: 'This desk for five minutes.'

- Avoid confrontational body language. You need to appear resolute not aggressive. A firm statement followed by walking away confirms your expectations.

- Voice: tone should be calm and clear.

- Avoid ambiguous questions, such as 'John would you go and sit at that desk?'. Some pupils will act or answer this literally; for example, 'No I can't or won't'.

- Continuing non-compliance results in a choice of increasing the consequences: 'John, if you choose not to work on your own, you will have to leave our classroom.' Provide one minute thinking time.

- Use the visual timer to prompt a response. Restart it if pupil is still non-compliant.

- Avoid discussions at all costs. You can return to level 2 choices as soon as the consequences have happened: 'Well done John, now that I can see you can work quietly, you can either go back to your group or stay and finish this on your own.' This allows the pupil to start making the right choices again and keeps everyone else focused on learning.

## Loss of privileges

'Mary you have chosen to go on messing around and your work is not finished. You can use five minutes of your break time to finish off the last question then you can go out.'

- Be realistic and take away small chunks of privilege rather than all of them. Take it all and you leave no room for the pupil to save face. If you take away too much, you may build resentment and confrontation. You similarly have nothing in reserve should you need it later. Additionally, total loss of break time as a consequence can make your next lesson (or someone else's) difficult because the pupil has had no respite.

- Make the consequences achievable, relevant and fixable. Demanding all course work be completed in one detention is just impossible and again makes moving forward uninviting.

- If the pupil has messed about all lesson, you are also responsible for letting that happen. Without 'beating oneself up' (there may well be good reason for your not tackling it earlier), remember this and maintain a level of personal responsibility in this.

- Look for opportunities to restore pupil responsibility for making the right choices: 'Mary I'm pleased you accepted loss of some of your break time and have caught up with your work; you can go out now.' This repairs your relationship and reinforces the pupil's belief that even when they make mistakes, they should and can put them right.

- Avoid endings that revisit the unwanted behaviour in a negative way, such as 'Well at least you've finished the work. If only you didn't mess about so much, you could do so much better.' This just reminds the pupil of the negative behaviour and reinforces all the wrong messages. It also prevents repair of your relationship.

## Thinking time (or time out approaches)

'John, five minutes thinking time to calm down and make the right choice.'

- This should be a technique used to create less pressure and more space to respond calmly. It is therefore of benefit to all parties involved in a brewing confrontation, including the teacher.

- Thinking time should be exactly that, thinking time, and away from the pressure that has led to the wrong behaviour occurring.

- Thinking time recognizes that space is needed to prevent reaching a point of no return. Time should be used to move things forward. It is a way of being able to consider a higher level consequence.

- It is not strictly a consequence in its own right and an appropriate consequence may need to follow the time out. Thinking time does mark a point of potential new direction, however.

- It recognizes that one or other party involved in the conflict needs space to work out what to do next.

- It needs to be in a space away from distractions and of very limited length, often five minutes maximum, before the next move is made. Lengthy time outs tend to breed resentment, not resolution. At best a sense of escape rather than facing responsibility is created.

- Time out cards can be written by the teacher and handed to the learner. They are used to indicate the decision being made by the teacher who has already offered the student choices.

- It should be dictated by the teacher. Avoid at all costs having a thinking time that is only limited in time by the compliance of the pupil: 'You can stay there until you are ready to apologize.' That may never happen and not facing the responsibility for their behaviour may be just what the student wants.

- It should have a timescale that is absolutely clear. Avoid at all costs having a thinking time that will end at some undefined moment in the future. Undefined timescales have little effect: 'When you stop shouting I will let you out' instead use 'Time out for five minutes'.

- Expecting work to be completed alone in a 'time out' situation can be contrary to the purpose of thinking time, that is, release of pressure. It may be the work is the pressure and having to do work alone may increase rather than decrease the stress. Completion of work may well have to happen, but after the time out where it can be successfully supported.

- It needs to enable students to focus on what they need to do in order to do the right thing. Getting students to write down what they did wrong, and why, must be avoided. This serves to reinforce their image as someone who gets it wrong and asking why is both accusatory and unproductive. Structure the student thinking time around 'It's gone wrong. How can you fix it?'

## Internal exclusion

Clearly this consequence brings into play whole-school approaches and is available only where suitable procedures and facilities are in place.

There are times, however, when some pupils need to be removed from the learning situation for a period of time beyond thinking time and this requires both immediate and well planned responses.

So when might internal exclusion be appropriate?

- Extreme outbursts of unacceptable behaviour.

- Prolonged series of lower level but constant behaviour that prevents the learning of others. This continues to occur despite all other level 1, 2 and 3 responses being deployed and is occurring in several areas of the curriculum.

Principles of effective use of internal exclusion include:

● Some behaviours are totally unacceptable and will result in pupils not being allowed to learn with their peers.

● Continued refusal to respond to level 1, 2 and 3 responses will lead to internal exclusion.

● All staff need to be clear about the expectations surrounding use of internal exclusion.

● Learning should continue and work set should be achievable with little supervision. This is not an 'alternative provision' but a consequence of very poor behaviour.

● A planned return to normal classes should be clear at the outset.

● The reason for the exclusion should be made clear to the pupil and that the next step will be a formal school exclusion.

● The decision to internally exclude should be part of a procedure that is swift in response but overseen by senior management and it is their job to ensure that the decision to internally exclude is consistently applied throughout the school.

● Use of internal exclusion must be about only the failure of the pupil to respond to all other levels of learning management not the failure of staff to apply these effectively.

● Periods of time should be between 0.5 to 2 days maximum.

● Non-co-operation in internal exclusion will need to result in formal exclusion.

● Entry and exit interviews need to be carefully conducted and include discussions about what the pupil is going to do in order to return successfully to lessons.

## External exclusion

While this may be the ultimate sanction, it is very rarely a real consequence for the student. Remember, in many cases the pupil is quite deliberately trying to avoid learning and excluding them from school can be a satisfying result in their eyes.

Exclusion can be a powerful consequence when used sparingly and briefly. Lengthy exclusions, that is, anything longer than a week, are counter-productive. All too often, longer exclusions only provide respite from learning and credibility and notoriety for the individual concerned.

Exclusion usually lacks any restoration. In other words, the student is not usually expected to make good what they have done wrong. This removes the students from taking responsibility for their actions. This is especially so when you choose to exclude pupils from school over several days. Restoring justice several days or weeks after the event loses its impact. This is why this form of consequence is highly undesirable and best avoided, wherever possible, through proper application of the level 1 and 2 processes.

Once exclusion has been used, it is important to avoid the temptation to frequently go over the catalogue of misdemeanours. Re-entry plans need to focus entirely on where we go from here. Re-entries after exclusion need to focus on ensuring the student has sufficient level 1 and 2 support in place when they return. It is about them returning to feeling safe and secure in the learning environment.

## The restoration process

The restoration process has already been briefly mentioned a number of times. That pupils, in some way, put right what they have done wrong is critical to their taking responsibility for their actions. It ensures that a process of learning occurs to support different responses in the future.

What follows is an example of a conversation that includes reference to focusing pupils on responsibility for their actions, facing consequences and restoring the harm done.

> Background: the pupil has become frustrated with his schoolwork in class. Despite attempts by the teacher to support him at level 1 and 2, he loses his cool and throws a pencil box – the box breaks and damages the wall. The pupil has had some thinking time and is now calmer.

| | |
|---|---|
| **Teacher** | Thanks for taking some thinking time, now we can begin to move on. |
| **Pupil** | But it weren't my fault; Daniel annoyed me and… |
| **Teacher** | I'm sure there are loads of things that led to this but now I'm interested in how you can put things right. |
| **Pupil** | What about my side of the story? |
| **Teacher** | What about the broken pencil case and the dent in the wall? |
| **Pupil** | Sorry but… |
| **Teacher** | We all make mistakes but what matters is how you put them right. Sorry doesn't fix the wall. |
| **Pupil** | OK I guess I need to replace the pencil box and ask the caretaker to help with the dent in the wall. |
| **Teacher** | Spot on, that's a good way forward! |

This dialogue is a briefer version of what might be said. It can take time to teach pupils to let go of their excuses and face their responsibilities. However, this investment does pay off in the mid- and long-term. While being a logical end to a serious breach of expectations, the restoration approach can have a significant effect in re-educating the responses a child has to stimuli in their environment. It sends the message that evasion through poor behaviour always results in having to face up to the issue in the end.

## The overview

To conclude this chapter, it is important to reiterate the significance of operating consistent, sequential approaches to managing behaviour when it fails to meet the expectations set.

Opposite are some examples of the kinds of responses to typical student behaviours at each of the three levels, including some suggestions of an appropriate restoration task.

| Student behaviour | Level 1 cueing | Level 2 choices | Level 3 consequences | Restoration process |
|---|---|---|---|---|
| 'This work is rubbish!' | 'I know it's not exciting but just make a start and see what you can do.' | 'If you are struggling, maybe working with John would help. You can either go it alone or work with John.' | 'You have not made the right choice. The consequences are detention this lunchtime.' | Work is completed, they lost their free time. |
| Taps pen on the table irritating other students. | Stand beside student and non-verbally indicate to put the pen down. | 'Either put the pen down on your table or mine.' | 'Pen on my table. Thank you.'<br><br>Non-compliance, take time out. | 'Earlier you disturbed the class. What can you do to put that right? Use five minutes of break tidying the book corner.' |
| Rocks on chair as a way of gaining attention. | Use the 'teacher look'!<br><br>Thank you when he stops. | 'Sit correctly on the chair or work in isolation.' | 'You are the weakest link goodbye!'<br>Or other face-saving exit strategy. | Something similar to above. |
| 'Stuff your f…ing lesson.' | | | Totally unacceptable behaviour, leave the room. | Opportunity for an active apology. A task that will benefit the person insulted. |

# Extreme behaviour

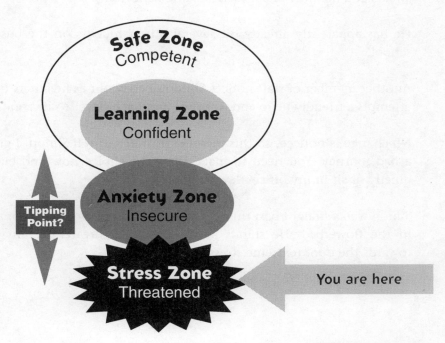

*The Learning Zone Model*

We have previously looked at the types of behaviour and responses that tend to occur in an accumulative way. There are, however, times when some students begin school and remain the whole day in the stress zone. Their behaviour may not be triggered entirely by school. Their behaviours can be really extreme and appear wild and out of control.

Some of these students come with labels or statements, some are from special units or special schools and some are already in our mainstream settings. Occasionally some students who are ordinarily fine, tip into the extreme end of the stress zone through some form of crisis. In these situations, we can find ourselves dealing with intense emotional outbursts and extreme physical behaviours.

The route back from the high stress zone can only be via the safe zone. Once we have tipped into the stress zone, no rational thinking can take place. The reptilian brain function is dominant and reasoning is over-ridden (refer to Chapter 2). Once in the stress zone, we start to act in ways we would not normally choose to do and revert to defensive/aggressive behaviours to defend our corner with no regard to what makes sense. This is not the same as being out of control; in fact it is more akin to old habits taking over our conscious control. This makes managing such crisis behaviour all the more challenging, as many of the behaviours are old, learned responses that may appear calculated and deliberate. To this end they can potentially trigger stress responses in us too.

To gain some practical insight into these scenarios consider the following situation.

Simon arrives in school in an extreme stress zone state and proceeds to reject all supportive measures offered at levels 1, 2 and 3.

The situation unfolds as follows.

Simon walks into the school building and immediately, without provocation, swears at a member of staff (stress zone behaviour).

He has apparently already hit several other students on the bus travelling into school.

Another member of staff notices Simon's behaviour as he enters the building and attempts a friendly hello and welcome approach (level 1 safe zone establishment).

No change is noticed, so this member of staff says 'Hi Simon, I guess you've had a bad journey. You need to make the right choice now and either go to class quietly or sit in my office' (level 2 choices).

Simon walks straight past this teacher back outside the front door and finds a rock in the flowerbed. He stands at the entrance threatening anyone who walks towards the door (extreme stress zone behaviour).

In this difficult situation, teachers need to be aware that this kind of behaviour:

- is the result of a primitive part of the brain and this is a child in real crisis.
- may appear very deliberate.
- will trigger your reptilian brain and set off your own stress responses.
- does not follow logic and rarely responds to logic.
- will threaten you personally both emotionally and potentially physically.
- may threaten other pupils and force you towards defending them.
- can be accumulative but is often unpredictable.

There are simple principles for dealing with really challenging situations. Students in extreme stress states need to:

- be rescued from their panic state.
- be rescued from the gaze and potential antagonism of others.
- be prevented from doing others harm, preferably through the removal of other people from the scene.
- be given space to calm down and may need to be given reassurance of safety.
- feel safe and secure before facing the consequences of their behaviour.
- resolve the consequences of their behaviour restoratively.

When a student is in this state of mind, the key is to allow the crisis moment to pass. When they are back in the safe zone, and only then, they can begin to process the outcomes of their actions.

## Behaviour that challenges persistently

Occasionally, there are children whose behaviour does not respond to the approaches described so far. These are rare circumstances. There is a most useful approach that can support you in rational analysis of such situations and is based on a behaviourist approach to creating solutions.

Based on the theories of behaviourists Skinner and Pavlov, the ABC Approach has become more sophisticated and much more practical for classroom use. The ABC Approach serves as a useful way to analyse what is needed when children challenge us and also brings a degree of objectivity to the situation. This objectivity is vital in situations where our own emotional responses may be clouding our judgement. We need to be objective about this in the sense that we may need to examine our own practice, without beating ourselves up! At the same time we need to be open to the possibility that changing our approach will change that of our students.

## The ABC Approach

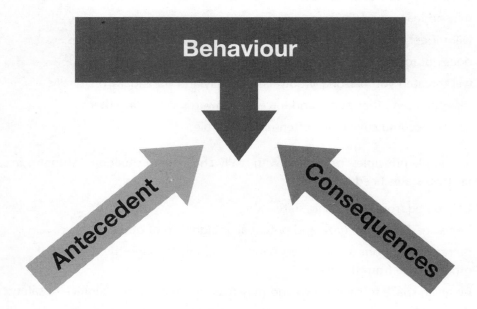

*The ABC Model*

**A = Antecedent**     This is best described as the 'trigger' for the subsequent 'B' – behaviour. It is what happens before the behaviour occurs – hence the title 'Antecedent'. Our focus should be on what we do to promote the right kind of behaviours. Appropriate antecedents stimulate good learning behaviours, inappropriate ones trigger poor learning behaviours.

**B = Behaviour**     Refocus this in the positive to move things forward and be clear about what you really want. This is about stating the behaviour that you want.

**C = Consequences**     That is, what is done in response to or immediately after the behaviour is observed. How you reinforce the right behaviour so it is more likely to occur again is the focus of consequences. Clearly this links into the consequences already discussed in this book.

## Key points about the ABC

- The ABC framework enables you to audit and rationalize challenging situations in school.

- Paying attention to the Antecedents (what happens before a behaviour occurs), the Behaviour itself and the Consequences (both rewards and sanctions) puts you back in control and gives you time to think about promoting learning behaviours rather than focusing on the unwanted behaviours.

- The starting point for managing learning behaviour is to focus on what you want to achieve. Future-basing (asking students to go into the future in their mind to a time when they have what they want to achieve) is an effective method of defining what you want, while avoiding unhelpful negative self-talk.

Use ABC to explore and resolve persistent misbehaviour. It is often the case that by examining and changing the way we set up our classroom, activities and responses we can promote positive learning behaviours. Using the ABC Approach with other supportive adults is a powerful way to approach positive change.

## Summary

- There are three levels of strategy for managing learning behaviours:
  → Cueing
  → Choices
  → Consequences.
- These levels allow us to deal appropriately with everyday consistent maintenance, to be flexible and pre-emptive when students approach tipping point and to manage high-level crises in classrooms.
- This chapter contains numerous strategies to choose from, at each level of intervention.
- Restoration is an important last step following consequences. It means students take responsibility for their actions.
- There are simple principles for dealing with children with really extreme behavioural responses.
- The ABC Approach is a way of analysing particularly difficult or unusual behaviour in children and it puts you back in control.

## Self-coaching insight questions

- How is your current practice making use of the three levels of intervention?
- Which strategies do you already use effectively?
- Which strategies do you intend to use in the near future?
- What are you learning about the appropriate use of these strategies in your classroom or your school?

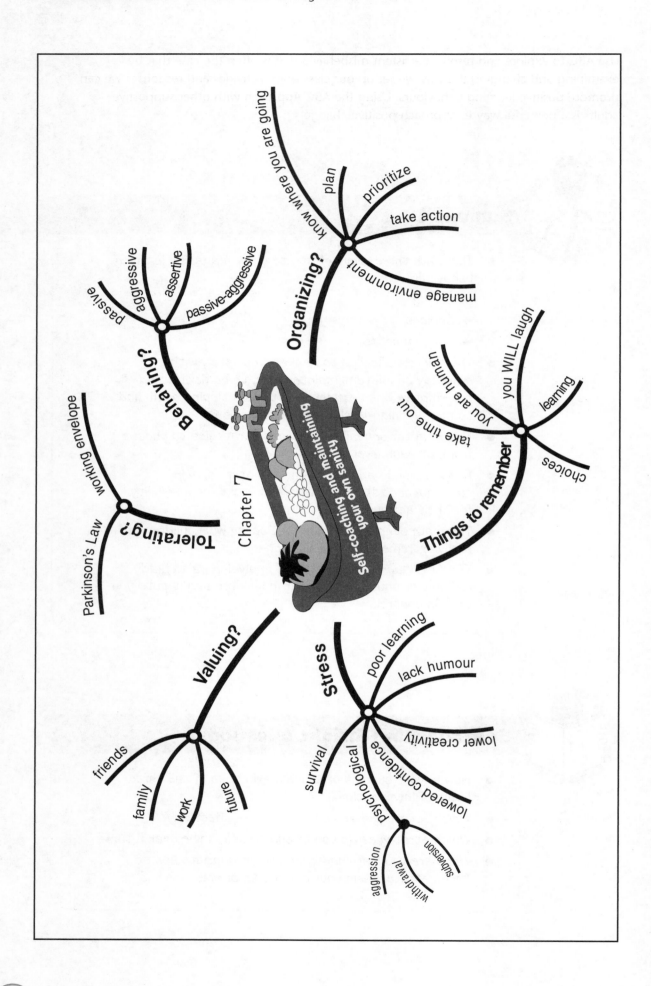

## Chapter 7

# Self-coaching and maintaining your own sanity

## Will Thomas

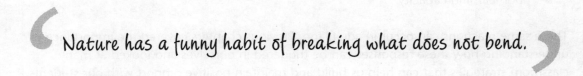

*Nature has a funny habit of breaking what does not bend.*

## In this chapter you will:

- acknowledge that you are human and that this is acceptable in school.
- explore ways to manage your own emotional and physiological reactions.
- understand how looking after yourself actually supports effective learning and behaviour.

## Preview questions

- What are you currently tolerating in your home or school life?
- What is the impact of these tolerations on you?
- What internal resources have you used in the past to help you to cope in crises?
- How are you currently looking after yourself
  - physically?
  - mentally?
  - emotionally?

Have you ever felt on the edge of despair in relation to your work? Have you ever felt that the pressures are just too great and the workload too high? If you have, then you will recognize some of the changes that occur in you along the way.

Stress takes a tremendous toll on schools. The impact of negative stress on students in classrooms has already been discussed at length. It is characterized by:

- physiological changes associated with survival
- psychological responses that can be aggressive, withdrawing or subversive
- the sapping of confidence
- the inhibition of creativity
- the absence of humour and enjoyment
- poor learning capacity.

These same reactions can occur in adults too. Previous chapters covered the importance of understanding how these responses can be triggered in ourselves and looked at many classroom strategies that can help us build and maintain positive rapport with our students. If we come into the classroom bringing high levels of anxiety and stress, then we will generate this out to our students.

We tend to mirror people, especially if they are our leaders. So when teachers, whether knowingly or unknowingly, bring their own 'issues' into the classroom, children pick it up. This chapter is designed to support you to handle some of the pressures on you more effectively – because teachers are human beings, with feelings and lives and other such realities!

When times are tough, here are some points to remember:

- You always have choices.
- There's more to life than school.
- Failure is just an opportunity to learn something new.
- One day soon you WILL laugh about this!
- You are human, and you might not get the balance right every time – give yourself a break.
- If you don't know what to do next, take time out.

It is easy to be hard on ourselves when we make mistakes and react rather than respond.

## Prevention is better than cure

Once you have shown your frustrations to your class, you are modelling for them behaviours you would not want to see them exhibit. Consequently, preventing those behaviours from arising is a crucial foundation. Having a good work–life balance can really support you to be resourceful, calm and measured in your classroom. It can enable you to have the resilience to cope with challenging behaviour in others and be even more objective.

There are five key areas to address in relation to work–life balance:

1   What are you valuing?
2   What are you tolerating?
3   How are you behaving?
4   How are you organizing?
5   How are you looking after yourself?

We will now explore each area in turn.

## What are you valuing?

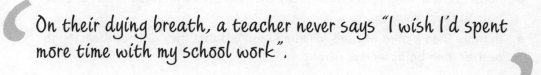

*On their dying breath, a teacher never says "I wish I'd spent more time with my school work".*

Something to think about.

### Friends, family, work and futures
We juggle many balls each day, our friends, our family, our professional responsibilities and our aspirations for the future.

Up in the air the balls go, over and down. Some we can throw really high and still catch, others we keep close to us. Every so often we drop balls and they hit the ground. Some balls are the ones made of high-density rubber and they spring back high in the air and back into our hands. Others drop with a dull thud and stay there until at some point we pick them up. No harm done. Some balls, however, are made of crystal and as they fall and hit the ground, they shatter.

● Which are the rubber balls in your life?
● Which are the ones that hang around until we pick them up again?
● Which balls are the crystals, the gems, that once dropped are never the same again?

If we give insufficient time to our nearest and dearest, it can lead to the erosion of the support that those people offer us. Valuing and honouring our close personal relationships is an important way of keeping ourselves resourceful and strong. If we allow crystal to shatter, it can destabilize many things including our jobs and career.

## What are you tolerating?

We can talk ourselves into believing that we cannot effect change; yet, when we look again, we realize we really can influence our own destiny ... so when will you act?

Consider this.

Parkinson's Law: 'Work expands to fill the time you make available to it.'

This means that the longer you are prepared to push the boundaries of work into the rest of your life, the more work will spill into your personal time.

An essential goal for anyone serious about reining in their hours at work is to create and use a working envelope.

## Some sobering facts

The DfEE (CIPD) work–life balance survey 2000 found that of those workers who worked more than 48 hours per week:

- 70 per cent of long-hours workers were too tired to hold a conversation.
- 43 per cent of partners of long-hours workers were 'fed up' with having to shoulder the domestic burdens.
- 29 per cent of partners of long-hours workers felt that the long hours had a 'quite or very negative effect' on their partner's relationship with their children.
- 56 per cent of long-hours workers say they have dedicated too much of their time to their work.
- In more than a third of cases, children reported that they did not see enough of their long-hours worker parent.

The effects of long hours working also impact on the effectiveness of individuals in their work role itself. If you work long and late, you are likely to be irritable and easily riled in the classroom. The working envelope represents an important checkpoint for you to work to.

## Making the envelope

How much time do you want to spend each week working?

This is a highly individual matter and depends on so many parameters in your life. You may have some unrealistic expectations! It is important to keep in mind that teaching is a profession that demands time from you beyond the confines of your contact time with pupils. You need to feel you have this time under control if you are to balance your life.

It may be important for you to set challenging targets for reducing your working envelope. It is vital, however, that you build in realistic timescales for reducing workload.

If your work is currently overwhelming you, there may be a number of key areas to work on. These matters may take some time to address, so be kind to yourself and give yourself reasonable timescales for change. The result of setting unreasonable demands is often disappointment and, consequently, loss of resilience.

Define your envelope as follows.

1. Be clear about how much time you are contractually expected to work over a year.
2. How many hours do you typically work per week? (Include before work, after work, at home, at weekends and in the holidays.)
3. Total up the hours you spent above this contractual obligation.
4. Consider how much time you are really satisfied to put in each week.
5. Decide on a working envelope for a week.
6. Plot the time you will spend working and where that time is spent on the grid opposite.

# Working envelope grid

| Time | Monday | Tuesday | Wednesday | Thursday | Friday | Saturday | Sunday |
|------|--------|---------|-----------|----------|--------|----------|--------|
| 6:00 | | | | | | | |
| 7:00 | | | | | | | |
| 8:00 | | | | | | | |
| 9:00 | | | | | | | |
| 10:00 | | | | | | | |
| 11:00 | | | | | | | |
| 12:00 | | | | | | | |
| 13:00 | | | | | | | |
| 14:00 | | | | | | | |
| 15:00 | | | | | | | |
| 16:00 | | | | | | | |
| 17:00 | | | | | | | |
| 18:00 | | | | | | | |
| 19:00 | | | | | | | |
| 20:00 | | | | | | | |
| 21:00 | | | | | | | |
| 22:00 | | | | | | | |

Consider this over a few days and tweak until you are content with it. Now sign a contract with yourself here.

This is my working envelope: _____

Having met the term 'work–life balance', I would like to emphasize the following important concept:

> We don't actually achieve balance but achieve balan*cing*.

Many of us try but fail to juggle our priorities because when we achieve a success we allow ourselves to give up the strategies that got us there. The moment of balance is lost. We quickly fall back to a position of imbalance.

When we commit to making a difference to our lives, then we commit to work–life balan*cing*. This involves setting very specific work–life balance goals and cultivating the behaviours that bring personal and professional effectiveness. There is no endpoint; it is ongoing actions that keep us balancing over time.

## How are you behaving?

Our approach to others affects our ability to influence them and this can be particularly important in communicating our work–home boundaries. We need to respond carefully and purposefully to colleagues who make unreasonable demands on us. The expectations of others can push us out of the work–life balance we hope for.

Essentially, there are four types of interaction behaviour that we use with others:

- passive
- aggressive
- assertive
- passive-aggressive.

Passive, aggressive and assertive behaviour all have their uses. Passive-aggressive behaviour is an unhelpful pattern for ourselves and others.

### Passive behaviour

The general characteristics of passive behaviour are:

- compliance
- resigned to fate
- pleasant
- self-critical
- pessimistic.

The downside of this behaviour is:

- a danger of being victimized
- being overworked
- losing self-respect
- quietly seeking the attention of others
- stirring anger in others
- being lead into boredom and lack of fulfilment.

The upside of this behaviour is:

- it is low risk
- it appears modest
- it avoids danger
- it is safe
- it uses discretion.

Use this type of behaviour to:

- melt into the background
- show modesty
- allow others to take the lead.

## Aggressive behaviour

The general characteristics of aggressive behaviour are:

- dominance
- forcefulness
- mistrust
- criticism of others
- impatience
- being status-hungry.

The downside of this behaviour is that it:

- can be abusive
- encourages others to be aggressive
- can make others feel threatened
- harbours destructive emotions
- can damage relationships in the long term.

The upside of this behaviour is that it:

- allows us to express genuine anger
- can work well in crisis situations
- gets you noticed
- can get you what you need quickly.

Use this type of behaviour to:

- defend yourself verbally under extreme pressure
- show your anger
- get noticed.

USE SPARINGLY AND BE IN CONTROL – IT GIVES UNPREDICTABLE RESULTS! It is unlikely to produce positive results in a classroom!

## Assertive behaviour

The general characteristics of assertive behaviour are:

- fairness
- sensitivity
- respect for others
- reflectiveness
- optimism.

The downside of assertive behaviour is that it:

- exerts limited power
- can make you disliked by others for expressing your needs.

The upside of assertive behaviour is that it:

- is independent
- is democratic and effective at maintaining sound relationships
- enables managed risks to be taken
- respects others
- helps you get others to support your goals.

Use this type of behaviour to:

- be decisive
- effectively communicate your point
- handle criticism
- negotiate
- communicate your needs while respecting those of others.

Assertive behaviour is a way of being clear about your needs without imposing them upon others. You should be assertive when:

- you are happy to reveal your thoughts and needs.
- you are looking to maintain healthy relationships.
- others are impinging on your time or your rights.

Behaving assertively will not always get you what you want or need, but it will enable you to make your needs clear and stand up to others who overstep your boundaries. It is essential in managing workload that you behave assertively if you are to maintain your working envelope.

Whatever the circumstances, you always have choices about how you behave. Experimenting with a variety of responses in different situations helps you to learn what works well, depending on the person and the situation.

# How are you organizing?

Personal organization is key to maintaining a healthy work–life balance. There are many approaches to getting and staying organized. In this section, the following key principles are outlined:

1  Know where you are going.
2  Plan your day, week, month and year.
3  Prioritize.
4  Take decisive action.

## 1 Know where you are going

Be absolutely clear what your goals are for the year, the term, the week and the day. Define how you will know when you have achieved them and what the benefits are of accomplishing them. A little time spent on being clear about what you are aiming for has great knock-on effects for keeping focused and on track.

## 2 Plan your day, week, month and year

Do this in reverse order. Decide what your goals are for the year. Consider them across your whole life: family and friends, school, career development, finance, health, leisure, personal development, intimate relationships, spirituality and so on. Decide what you want and then divide these into sub-goals to work towards each month, week and ultimately each day. Spend a few minutes each week reflecting on these goals and what you need to do to keep moving towards them.

## 3 Prioritize

Once you have defined your goals, it is then much easier to prioritize the tasks that come your way. Not everything that comes into our lives is a priority. When we wrongly prioritize some things over others, we can unbalance ourselves. If we fail to prioritize, we become reactive rather than proactive and sometimes the trivial overrides the really important.

Keeping a log each day for a week of how you use your time can help to show patterns of inappropriate prioritization. Though it initially takes time to do, it will reveal fascinating information that will help you improve your effectiveness.

A simple and very effective way to manage priorities is to use an URGENT–IMPORTANT grid as shown overleaf. You can use the grid to identify the nature of a task on your list.

| Urgent and Important (UI) | Non-Urgent but Important (NUI) |
|---|---|
| Crisis management<br>Problems<br>Some behaviour management issues<br>Other people's lack of planning | Communication<br>Building teams<br>Planning ahead<br>Anticipating issues and preparing<br>Learning and preparing to enhance it<br>Rest and recuperation<br>Providing feedback to learners |
| **Urgent but Not Important (UNI)** | **Non-Urgent and Not Important (NUNI)** |
| Some interruptions<br>Some email/snail mail<br>Some other people's priorities | Quite a lot of email and snail mail<br>Low level paperwork<br>Bemoaning the teacher's lot<br>Timewasters |

Get into the habit of considering the urgency and importance of each task as you put it onto your weekly or daily 'To Do list'. If it is not a UI or a NUI, then lower it in your priorities or strike it out altogether. Non-Urgent but Important (NUI) tasks are the ones that relate to your longer-term goals. Actually prioritizing working on these is really important as it keeps you moving in the direction you planned and reduces blind reactivity.

## 4 Take decisive action

Procrastination is avoiding taking action. It is characterized by a whole series of avoidance behaviours that put work off. For example, chatting in the staffroom rather than going and marking that set of books, which would mean you would have no work to take home that evening!

We can put off doing tasks for a number of reasons:

- there are emotional difficulties attached to a task.
- the task is large or complex and we have not considered the steps involved.
- the task involves interacting with someone we fear or see as difficult to work with.
- the job is uninspiring, requires a low level of skill, or does not seem to have a direct impact on improving learning.

The following are typical tasks that cause people to procrastinate. Each one is followed by some tips for taking decisive action.

- *Big or complex jobs* – spend some time breaking these into a series of smaller tasks and plan when you will do each sub-task. For example, planning a set of lessons for a new syllabus.
- *High-level cognitively challenging tasks* – do these when you have your highest energy levels in the day – avoid late afternoon. For example, understanding complex concepts and deciding how to teach them.

- *Low level, repetitive tasks* – work on these when you have low levels of energy. This can actually make these tasks more rewarding. For example, simple marking or making resources.
- *Emotionally challenging tasks* – predict the likely challenges and plan a range of assertive ways to deal with them. Ask others to help you think it through. For example, planning how to deal with the behaviour of a challenging student.

Below are some general tips on dealing with procrastination.

- Tackle the thing on your task list you most want to avoid, first!
- *Get started*. Do something, anything, to get the ball rolling when you recognize yourself procrastinating. For example, clear your desk of everything except one simple task and do it there and then.
- *Manage the complaining culture*. In schools there can be a culture of complaining about how bad things are. At a low level, this can serve to acknowledge the strains of teaching, but if allowed to be the focus of interaction with others, it can lock you into a negative thinking cycle. Acknowledge the difficulties and move on. For example, choose carefully who to spend time with during lunches and breaks; shift negative conversations to positive with a focus on humorous or successful events.

If you have a persistent problem with procrastination, the services of a personal coach can be useful to help you break the patterns of behaviour that lead to it. Look for a coach who uses NLP coaching techniques.

## How are you looking after yourself?
### Maintaining resilience
We have an internal resilience bank account. When we continue to draw on our resilience bank account without putting anything back in, our account becomes overdrawn. This overdraft leads to stress, reduced performance, negative emotions, damaged relationships and, eventually, ill health. Over a long period it can shorten your life.

There are inevitably times of unexpected demand in your role. These will draw on your reserves and can actually be exciting. However, if you have few reserves within you, then you will begin to experience all demands as negative stress. Taking care of our physical and mental health is important for our longer-term health and happiness and, of course, it has an impact on our ability to be effective in our classroom.

### Looking after your mental health
Minimize stress by:

- planning ahead for the long, medium and short term.
- blocking out planning and relaxation time each week and taking it.
- being realistic with your plans.
- being flexible towards your plans and building in enough margin for coping with unexpected demands – a teacher will always have them!
- making lists and ticking off things you achieve – praise yourself.
- taking time out during the day – even a few seconds without stimulus can help psychologically.

- eating and drinking healthily, especially water (eight glasses per day) – your brain needs to be hydrated to work effectively. Irritability comes with dehydration.
- creating time for exercise and mental space.
- doing something for YOU each week, something you enjoy and look forward to.
- seeking help from others if you feel you are suffering from too much stress.

## Looking after your long-term health

A poor work–life balance has short-term effects on our ability to achieve deadlines and sustain relationships, and it also affects memory. Long term it can have real consequences for our health. An array of diseases is caused or intensified by stress, including cardio-vascular disease, immune problems, panic attacks, depression, ulcers and colitis.

A prescription that puts us in the right direction to short and longer-term health is R.E.S.T., which stands for:

# Refuel – eat and drink properly for maximum performance.

# Exercise – take regular exercise for posture, health and stamina.

# Stop – take stimulus-free time.

# Time – reflect on your successes and plan your next steps to aid work–life balance.

### Refuel

We hear a great deal in the news about obesity and poor diet. The figures suggest a nation eating inappropriately. A balanced diet of unprocessed foods with plenty of fruit and vegetables is at the heart of good health.

There is strong evidence now to link poor diet with life-threatening diseases, such as cancer and cardiovascular disease. It is well known that we need a balanced diet for long-term health. We now also know that what we eat and drink affects our mental as well as our physical well-being in more immediate ways:

*Teacher's fix*: caffeinated drinks, such as coffee, Coke and tea, cause our nerves to misfire and create alertness hyper-states. This affects sleep, creates irregular heart rates and feelings of anxiety. Cut back gradually for a couple of weeks and notice the benefits. Drink water instead.

*Teacher's famine*: going for long periods during the day without food leads our body to think it is facing famine. We develop low blood sugar levels leading to headaches, irritability and feeling low in energy. This can promote the deposition of fat when we next eat. Set some boundaries about eating well in school, stick to them and eat away from your desk!

*Teacher's rush*: eating high carbohydrate foods, such as chocolate and bread, create high sugar loads in our bloodstream in very short timeframes. Our body responds with high insulin release and over-zealous blood sugar reduction. A lack of energy follows the initial rush. We can feel extremely tired after sugary foods, and irritability and poor concentration follow. Avoid sugary foods such as chocolate and replace with slow release carbohydrates balanced with fat and protein.

Water makes up 80 per cent of our body and surrounds every cell in our body. Our cells carry out all the specialized functions in our body. Many work together to balance our internal chemistry.

Cells suffer when there is insufficient water available. You have only to think back to your last hangover to know the physical symptoms of dehydration! When we are dehydrated:

● cell energy production is compromised and headaches occur.

● brain cells are sensitive to dehydration and learning is impaired.

● we become irritable – this is one of the early signs of dehydration.

● the prolonged low water levels in the body can compromise kidney function.

When you are well hydrated, you quite literally feel great. Get into the habit of drinking water during the day and remember that caffeine actually exacerbates water loss – the more caffeine you take, the more water you need to drink.

## Exercise

Even moderate exercise is good for you. The British Heart Foundation (www.bhf.org.uk) recommend five sessions of exercise per week each lasting around 30 minutes. Exercise should raise your heart rate and breathing rate and make you feel a little warm.

Building in exercise is so beneficial because it:

● boosts feel-good chemical levels – endorphins and enkephalins.

● enhances concentration and alertness.

● encourages healthy functioning of the cardiovascular system.

● improves muscle and lung performance.

● supports healthier weight.

● helps you look and feel better, enhancing self-esteem.

Over two-thirds of us do less than the recommended amount of physical activity! A good blast after a testing time in the classroom can really re-energize you. Endorphins help you feel resourceful and you do not have to go to a gym to benefit. Choose an exercise that you will enjoy. One of the best exercises is just walking.

How could you bring more exercise into your day?

## Stop

Have we truly forgotten how to rest and provide ourselves with a low stimulus environment? Teachers may have in excess of 70 human interactions per hour in a typical day. That could mean as many as 500 interactions in one day!

When you finish your day, make time to reduce the number of stimuli. You could:

- meditate and clear your mind through focusing on your breathing.
- sit quietly and read the paper.
- close your eyes and think of being in your dream location.
- spend some time with someone you care about.
- spend some time with a pet.
- take a walk or some other form of gentle exercise.

## Time

Reflecting on progress is important in terms of improving how to approach tasks and situations in the future. It is also vital to review and celebrate your successes, which is part of the process of rest and renewal.

Here are some helpful approaches.

### Ring-fenced reflection

1 Switch off the part of you that considers what did not go so well.
2 Reflect on and list all of the successes – big and small – this week, term, year.
3 For each success identify the strengths you showed in achieving that success.
4 Take some time to reflect on your success and congratulate yourself.
5 File these and bring them out again when the going gets tough.

### Wider reflection

1 Consider what things did not go well.
2 What would make them run more smoothly in future?
3 What did you learn about yourself in this situation?
4 How does this new knowledge help you in the future?
5 Set a specific goal for improvement and add to your list of goals.

### The learning release

Whatever happened in your day, there is always some positive learning. Sitting quietly and allowing yourself to reflect on what positive learning can come from your experiences is a rewarding and helpful way to let go of stress and ease yourself into rest.

And above all remember that you deserve a break!

For a comprehensive set of tips and tools for managing workload, organization and effective approaches to saying 'no' at work, *The Managing Workload Pocketbook* (Thomas 2005) is a helpful reference (www.teacherspocketbooks.co.uk). The book leads you to a useful website with downloadable work–life balance tools.

## Summary

- Your performance in the classroom is positively affected by your resourcefulness and resilience.
- When we allow our resourcefulness and resilience to be compromised, it can affect our ability to respond appropriately to challenging student behaviour.
- Prevention is better than cure in respect of managing student behaviour and so looking after ourselves is important in being ready for the challenges of the classroom.
- Valuing our support networks is vital. This means taking time to support our family and friends, and other close relationships.
- Work expands to fill the time we make available to it. Set boundaries.
- We have choices about how we respond to others in relation to the expectations they place upon us.
- Knowing where we are going in terms of goals and aspirations informs how we prioritize work and helps prevent procrastination.
- R.E.S.T. is the prescription for good mental, emotional and physical health.

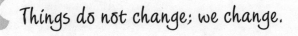

> *Our lives improve only when we take chances – and the first and most difficult risk we can take is to be honest with ourselves.*
>
> (Walter Anderson)

> *Things do not change; we change.*
>
> (Henry David Thoreau)

## Self-coaching insight questions

On a scale of one to ten, where one is not at all and ten is totally satisfied, work out your response to the following questions.

- How satisfied are you currently with your work–life balance?

- How satisfied are you with your current level of resilience and resourcefulness to deal with challenging behaviour in your classroom?

- How satisfied are you with the amount of rest and recuperation you are able to have on weekday evenings and weekends?

- How satisfied are you currently with your ability to say no to demands around you?

- How satisfied are you with the time you are giving to friends, family and other intimate relationships?

- How satisfied are you with your current clarity about your goals and aspirations for the next year?

- Finally, what action will you be taking as a first step to addressing any issues arising in this chapter?

If you would like further support with the issues in this chapter, you might like to consider further training or personal coaching. For more information visit www.visionforlearning.co.uk for details of personal coaching and training in workload management issues.

 *You must be the change you wish to see in the world.*

(Mahatma Gandhi)

# Recommended reading

Carter, R. (1998) *Mapping the Mind*, Seven Dials

Claxton, G. (2002) *Building Learning Power*, TLO

Claxton, G. (2006) *The Wayward Mind*, Abacus

Covey, S. (1989) *The Seven Habits of Highly Effective People*, Simon and Schuster

Dilts, R. (1990) *Changing Belief Systems with NLP*, Meta Publications

Goleman, D. (1995) *Emotional Intelligence: Why it can matter more than IQ*, Bloomsbury

Johnson, S. (1998) *Who Moved My Cheese?*, Vermillion

Kohn, A. (2000) *Punished by Rewards*, Houghton Mifflin

Long, R. (2005) *Better Behaviour*, David Fulton

Long, R. (2005) *Yeah Right! Adolescents in the Classroom*, David Fulton

Mahoney, T. (2003) *Words Work: How to Change your Language*, Crown House

Maines, B. and Robinson, G. (1997) *Even Better Parents Trainer Resource Pack*, Lucky Duck

McConnon, S. and McConnon, M. (2002) *Resolving Conflict*, Communicators

Persaud, R. (2005) *The Motivated Mind*, Bantam Press

Robertson, J. (1997) *No Need to Shout*, Folens Quick Guides

Rogers, B. (2000) *Behaviour Management: A Whole School Approach*, Paul Chapman

Rogers, B. (2002) *Classroom Behaviour: A Practical Guide to Effective Teaching*, Paul Chapman

Sapolsky, R. M. (1998) *Why Zebras don't get Ulcers*, Freeman

Slater, L. (2005) *Opening Skinner's Box*, Bloomsbury

Smith, A. (2004) *The Brain's Behind It*, Network Educational Press

Smith, A. and Call, N. (1999) *The ALPS Approach*, Network Educational Press

Smith, A., Lovatt, M. and Wise, D. (2003) *Accelerated Learning: A User's Guide*, Network Educational Press

Thomas, W. (2004) *Managing Workload Pocketbook*, Teachers' Pocketbooks

Thomas, W. (2005) *Coaching Solutions Resource Book*, Network Educational Press

Thomas, W. and Smith, A. (2004) *Coaching Solutions*, Network Educational Press

# Useful websites

| | |
|---|---|
| www.alite.co.uk | Alistair Smith's website – training and consultancy |
| www.behaviour4learning.ac.uk | Information about behaviour management |
| www.bhf.org.uk | British Heart Foundation website |
| www.brainconnection.com | International information on the brain |
| www.buildinglearningpower.co.uk | Training and consultancy on Building Learning Power |
| www.circle-time.co.uk | Jenny Mosley's website – positive classrooms |
| www.dfes.gov.uk/behaviourandattendance | DfES information on behaviour |
| www.learningsuccess.co.uk | Anne Copley's website – training and consultancy |
| www.luckyduck.co.uk | Resources for behaviour management and so on |
| www.onelifenetwork.co.uk | Will Smith's website |
| www.pz.harvard.edu | Learning Research at Harvard, includes resources |
| www.shirleyclarke-education.org | Shirley Clarke's website |
| www.teacherspocketbooks.co.uk | Useful publications for teachers |
| www.team-teach.co.uk | Training in care and control |
| www.tloltd.co.uk | Training and consultancy on Building Learning Power |
| www.visionforlearning.co.uk | Will Thomas website |

# Index

Note: The suffix 's' denotes a chapter summary.

# Network Continuum Education – much more than publishing...

## Network Continuum Education Conferences – Invigorate your teaching

Each term NCE runs a wide range of conferences on cutting edge issues in teaching and learning at venues around the UK. The emphasis is always highly practical. Regular presenters include some of our top-selling authors such as Sue Palmer, Mike Hughes and Steve Bowkett. Dates and venues for our current programme of conferences can be found on our website www.networkcontinuum.co.uk.

## NCE online Learning Style Analysis – Find out how your students prefer to learn

Discovering what makes your students tick is the key to personalizing learning. NCE's Learning Style Analysis is a 50-question online evaluation that can give an immediate and thorough learning profile for every student in your class. It reveals how, when and where they learn best, whether they are right brain or left brain dominant, analytic or holistic, whether they are strongly auditory, visual, kinesthetic or tactile… and a great deal more. And for teachers who'd like to take the next step, LSA enables you to create a whole-class profile for precision lesson planning.

Developed by The Creative Learning Company in New Zealand and based on the work of Learning Styles expert Barbara Prashnig, this powerful tool allows you to analyse your own and your students' learning preferences in a more detailed way than any other product we have ever seen. To find out more about Learning Style Analysis or to order profiles visit www.networkcontinuum.co.uk/lsa.

**Also available: Teaching Style Analysis and Working Style Analysis.**

## NCE's Critical Skills Programme – Teach your students skills for lifelong learning

The Critical Skills Programme puts pupils at the heart of learning, by providing the skills required to be successful in school and life. Classrooms are developed into effective learning environments, where pupils work collaboratively and feel safe enough to take 'learning risks'. Pupils have more ownership of their learning across the whole curriculum and are encouraged to develop not only subject knowledge but the fundamental skills of:

- problem solving
- creative thinking
- decision making
- communication
- management
- organization

- leadership
- self-direction
- quality working
- collaboration
- enterprise
- community involvement

'The Critical Skills Programme… energizes students to think in an enterprising way. CSP gets students to think for themselves, solve problems in teams, think outside the box, to work in a structured manner. CSP is the ideal way to forge an enterprising student culture.'

Rick Lee, Deputy Director, Barrow Community Learning Partnership

To find out more about CSP training visit the Critical Skills Programme website at www.criticalskills.co.uk